EARTH ALERT

Environmental Studies for Grades 4-6

by Denise Bieniek, M.S.
Illustrated by Dan Regan

Troll

CREATIVE
TEACHER
IDEAS

Troll Creative Teacher Ideas was designed to help today's dedicated, time-pressured teacher. Created by teachers for teachers, this innovative series provides a wealth of classroom ideas to help reinforce important concepts and stimulate your students' creative thinking skills.

Each book in the series focuses on a different curriculum theme to give you the flexibility to teach any given skill at any time of the year. The wide range of ideas and activities included in each book are certain to help you create an atmosphere where students are continually eager to learn new concepts and develop important skills.

We hope this comprehensive series will provide you with everything you need to foster a fun and challenging learning environment for your students. **Troll Creative Teacher Ideas** is a resource you'll turn to again and again!

Titles in this series:

Classroom Decor:
Decorate Your Classroom from Bulletin Boards to Time Lines

Creative Projects: Quick and Easy Art Projects

Earth Alert: Environmental Studies for Grades 4-6

Explore the World: Social Studies Projects and Activities

Healthy Bodies, Healthy Minds

Holidays Around the World: Multicultural Projects and Activities

It All Adds Up: Math Skill-Building Activities for Grades 4-6

Learning Through Literature:
Projects and Activities for Linking Literature and Writing

Story Writing: Creative Writing Projects and Activities

Think About It: Skill-Building Puzzles Across the Curriculum

The World Around Us: Geography Projects and Activities

World Explorers: Discover the Past

Metric Conversion Chart		
1 inch = 2.54 cm	1 foot = .305 m	1 yard = .914 m
1 mile = 1.61 km	1 fluid ounce = 29.573 ml	1 cup = .24 l
1 pint = .473 l	1 teaspoon = 4.93 ml	1 tablespoon = 14.78 ml

Contents

Outer Space Search

Name _____

Find the outer space words hidden in the puzzle below. The words may be written forward, backward, up, down, or diagonally.

```
U R C O N S T E L L A T I O N S P R
T E T Z A S T R A U T R M B R L Y O
U M U U P T Z G A R O C E O U X S P
A O A K C O M A R S T U N I T B T H
N N N R A T M O O A D H G K A I I K
U O O A B U D N S U V E N U S G R Y
T R E T I P U J U P L I T O M J E J
O T R Y G S O O R X H A T M I T O I
I S T T D M H T A G A E X Y L M I G
B A S T R O T E N A L P R M K L R P
C I A I Q O E C U E S U J E Y A S L
J Y G B U T U L S L P L U T W T G A
L T P D X A N C Y E F T B R A I N T
D U L O I N O O M E R C U R Y P D U
O F A L C P L U I T O R A N H L M P
C E R R E P P I L G I B T R E U B S
B I G D I P P E R T U A N O R T S A
G R V A Y X Y H Y X A L A G O O N M
```

astronaut	constellation	Jupiter	moon	Saturn	telescope
astronomer	Earth	Mars	Neptune	star	Uranus
atmosphere	galaxy	Mercury	planet	sun	Venus
Big Dipper	gravity	Milky Way	Pluto		

Solar System Model

MATERIALS:

flour
salt
water
bowls
blunt sewing needles
waxed paper
paints and paintbrushes
construction paper
markers
craft sticks
glue
strong thread
scissors

DIRECTIONS:

1. Divide the class into small groups. Have each group work at a separate table or work area.

2. Before they make the planets and the sun, have students do some research on the size of each one. For example, the sun, which is the largest body in the solar system, should be made the largest.

3. Distribute flour, salt, water, and bowls to each table. Instruct students to make some dough using equal parts of flour and salt mixed with water. Have them add water gradually, stirring until the mixture forms a ball and does not stick to hands.

4. Have each group roll a ball to represent the sun and continue dividing the dough and rolling planets until all nine are completed. Compare them to make sure the sizes are approximately correct in proportion to each other (for example, Earth should not be larger than Jupiter).

5. Push a blunt needle through each ball, about a quarter of the way from the edge. Place the balls on waxed paper.

6. When the balls are dry, have students paint them to resemble the surfaces of each planet and of the sun.

7. Create rings for planets when appropriate by cutting a ring from construction paper that is just large enough to fit around the planet snugly. With a marker, draw concentric circles to match the number of rings around a particular planet.

6

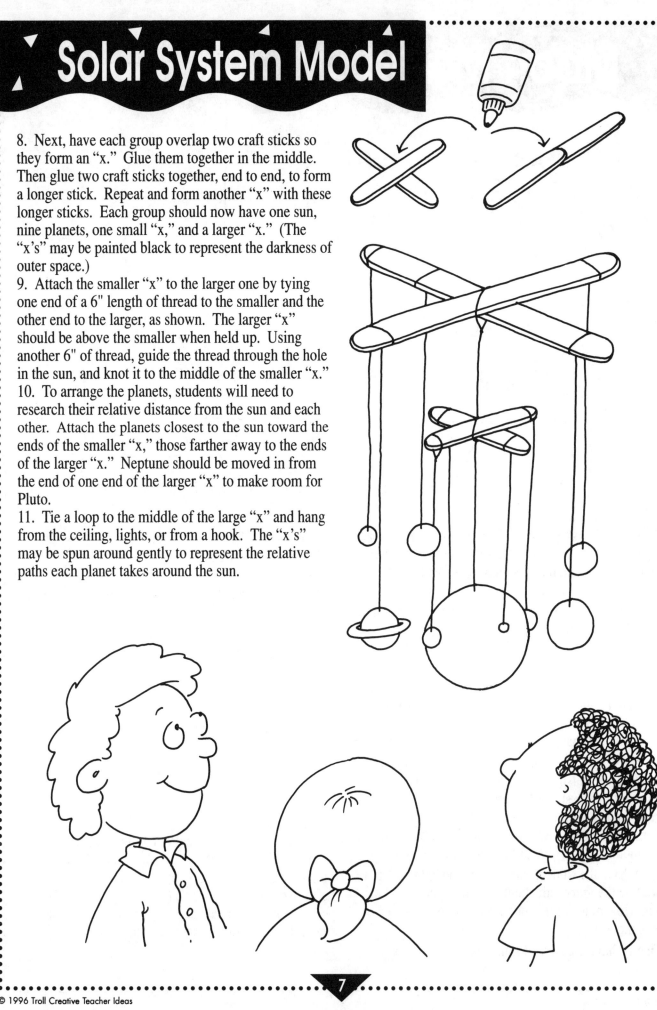

8. Next, have each group overlap two craft sticks so they form an "x." Glue them together in the middle. Then glue two craft sticks together, end to end, to form a longer stick. Repeat and form another "x" with these longer sticks. Each group should now have one sun, nine planets, one small "x," and a larger "x." (The "x's" may be painted black to represent the darkness of outer space.)

9. Attach the smaller "x" to the larger one by tying one end of a 6" length of thread to the smaller and the other end to the larger, as shown. The larger "x" should be above the smaller when held up. Using another 6" of thread, guide the thread through the hole in the sun, and knot it to the middle of the smaller "x."

10. To arrange the planets, students will need to research their relative distance from the sun and each other. Attach the planets closest to the sun toward the ends of the smaller "x," those farther away to the ends of the larger "x." Neptune should be moved in from the end of one end of the larger "x" to make room for Pluto.

11. Tie a loop to the middle of the large "x" and hang from the ceiling, lights, or from a hook. The "x's" may be spun around gently to represent the relative paths each planet takes around the sun.

Moon Mania

Ask students to observe the shape of the moon each night for a month and draw the moon shapes (crescent moon, half-moon, three-quarter moon, and full moon) they see on calendars.

Discuss any patterns students observed. Ask children to make predictions for the next month's cycle. Then have the students observe for another month to check their predictions.

Demonstrate the different phases of the moon using an unshaded light bulb and a grapefruit. Ask a student to stand about 3' from the lamp. Turn off all the lights and draw the shades.

Demonstrate to the student how to hold the grapefruit in his or her outstretched hand directly in line with the light bulb. The student is representing the Earth. The grapefruit is the moon and the light bulb is the sun. Turn the lamp on. Ask the student to see how much of the moon is lit. (None of it, which is a new moon.)

Next, have the student stand facing the light bulb but holding the grapefruit about 1' to the right of him or her. How much of the moon is lit? (Half, which is a half-moon.)

Finally, have the student stand with his or her back to the sun and hold the moon about 1' away and to the left. How much is visible now? (All of it, which is a full moon.)

After the demonstration, ask students some questions, such as:

> From where does the light on the moon come? (It is reflected light from the sun.)

> Does the moon change shape in each phase? (No, the only thing that changes is the way sunlight is reflected off the moon.)

> Name the phases of the moon. (Crescent, half-moon, three-quarter moon, full moon.)

You may also wish to demonstrate a solar eclipse. Use the lamp without a shade, a large playground ball, and a smaller ball. Place the larger ball about 2' from the lamp. Turn off all lights and close the shades. Ask one student to hold the smaller ball in an outstretched hand directly in line of the "sun" and the "Earth." Turn on the lamp. What happens to the portion of Earth that was formerly lit? (It becomes dark.) This phenomenon occurs about every 18 months and blocks sunlight from hitting certain parts of the Earth.

Earth Facts Crossword

Name _____

Fill in the Earth facts below to complete the crossword puzzle. Use an encyclopedia or a science book if you need help!

Across

2. The Earth is about 30% ___ .
4. The number of moons the Earth has.
6. It takes about 365 1/4 days for the Earth to ___ around the sun.
8. Wet, steamy tropical areas are called rain ___ .
10. Huge ice masses found on Earth are called ___ .
12. The distance between the ___ and the Earth is approximately 93 million miles.
13. The Earth is a part of this galaxy.
15. The theory that Earth's continents were formed by the slow movement of large land masses.
16. The name of the famous Polish astronomer who proved the Earth did not stand still while stars and other bodies circled it.

Down

1. The Earth is about 70% ___ .
3. Large stretches of very dry areas.
4. The main components of the Earth's atmosphere are nitrogen and ___ .
5. Tall masses of dirt and rock.
7. The ___ of the Earth causes day and night.
9. The force that holds things down.
11. The dirtying of Earth's land, water, and air.
14. The three main layers of Earth are the crust, the mantle, and the ___ .

Earth and Sun Experiments

MATERIALS:
globe
1" paper cutout of a person
flashlight

DIRECTIONS:
1. Try these classic experiments with the class. Ask for three volunteers. Tell the first student to look on a globe for the country in which he or she lives, and tape a 1" paper cutout of a person to that country.
2. Ask the second student to hold the globe and the third student to hold the flashlight. Then have the second student turn the globe so that the paper cutout points toward the student holding the flashlight.
3. With the lights out, instruct the third student to turn on the flashlight. Ask the class to name the continents that are experiencing daytime and the ones that are experiencing nighttime. Then have the student holding the globe turn it around very slowly until the paper cutout is nearest the student. Now have students tell which lands are having day and which are having night. Explain that the Earth is always spinning. It takes about 24 hours for the Earth to rotate once; it is this spinning that causes day and night.
4. An experiment to help the class understand seasons requires the same materials as above. Ask for two new volunteers, and have one hold the globe and the other hold the flashlight.
5. Have the other students form an ellipse around the two volunteers; this is the shape of Earth's path around the sun. Inform the class that besides rotating, the Earth also orbits the sun. It takes about 365 1/4 days for the Earth to complete its orbit; this is the length of one year.
6. Next, ask the student holding the globe to move around the sun inside the ellipse, keeping the cutout facing the sun. Point out that the Earth is on a tilt. When the northern half of Earth is tilted toward the sun during its orbit, those northern areas have summer. The southern half gets the sun at a lower angle and experiences winter. Have the students tell the volunteer holding the globe to stop when they think their region is having summer. Explain that six months later, the Earth's southern half is tilted toward the sun and has summer, while the northern half has winter. Have them stop him or her again when they think they are having winter.
7. Ask the class to name ways in which the sun affects our lives. Some answers may be: the sun gives plants the ability to perform photosynthesis; if green plants can perform photosynthesis, other animals in the food chain will survive; the sun provides people, animals, and plants with warmth; the sun provides us with light. Reinforce the fact that without the sun, no life would exist on Earth.

10

© 1996 Troll Creative Teacher Ideas

Earth Cake

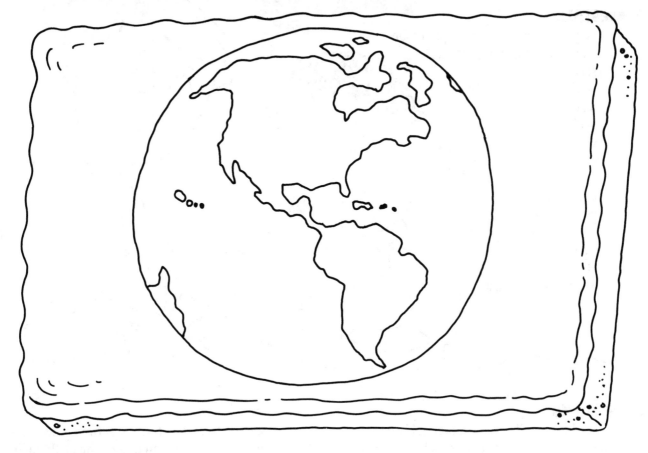

MATERIALS:

cake mix
mixing bowl
mixer
rectangular cake pan
plate or cookie sheet
vanilla frosting
blue and green food coloring
cake cutter and knife
plates and forks

DIRECTIONS:
1. Make the cake according to the directions on the back of the box, or follow your favorite homemade recipe. Pour the batter into a rectangular cake pan and bake.
2. When cool, transfer the cake to a plate or cookie sheet. Spread a thin layer of vanilla frosting on the top of the cake.
3. Place 2/3 of the remaining frosting in one bowl and add 10 drops of blue food coloring. Put the rest of the frosting in another bowl and add 6 drops of green food coloring. Looking at a picture of the Earth for reference, decorate the cake with the frosting, blue for water, green for land.
4. Before cutting the cake, ask each student to say one thing about the Earth that they find interesting or surprising. Then dig in and enjoy!

3-D Surface Map

MATERIALS:

very large cardboard box (preferably
   one from a new refrigerator)
scissors
world map
markers
wallpaper paste
water
mixing bowl
newspaper
toothpicks
green and blue
   construction paper
tape
glue
paint and paintbrushes

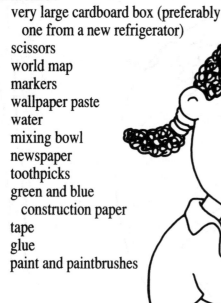

DIRECTIONS:

1. Obtain a large cardboard box, preferably one from a new refrigerator or other large household appliance. Cut one of the bigger sides from the box and lay it flat on a large surface, such as the floor or two tables pushed together.

2. Study a world map and transfer the countries onto the cardboard surface. This may be accomplished by copying the shapes of the land masses and bodies of water onto the cardboard. Or students may want to make tracings of the land and water, then glue them onto the cardboard. Try to make the transfer as large as possible.

3. Make a mixture of wallpaper paste and water. Add water to a cup or two of the paste until it forms a thick but pourable mixture.

4. Cut newspaper into strips, reserving some whole sheets.

5. To make mountains, crumble whole pieces of newspaper and tape them down to the appropriate spots. Dip strips of newspaper into the paste mixture, pulling each strip through two fingers to get the excess paste off. Lay the strips over the mountains and mountain ranges, smoothing the paste as you go.

6. To make rain forests, cut tree tops from green construction paper. Poke one end of a toothpick through the center of the construction paper and the other end through the cardboard in the appropriate places. (Use tape or glue to hold tree tops and trunks in place if necessary.)

7. When the newspaper is dry, paint the surface according to the particular features of the different areas. For example, plains may be painted green; frozen areas having glaciers may be painted white; mountains may be painted brown, black, or other appropriate colors. Oceans and other bodies of water may be painted blue or aqua.

8. Use markers to write out the names of the various countries, oceans, and larger lakes. Students may also want to identify other features with which they are familiar. For instance, if students wish to create a waterfall, they may glue or tape blue construction paper or cellophane to the top of a mountain or rise and fold it down into a river or lake.

9. Place the Earth's surface on display for other classes to view, as well as parents who visit the classroom.

Natural Forces

Discuss some of these important natural forces that affect the Earth's surface with the class. Afterward, ask each student to choose one of these forces to write about in a research paper.

Earthquakes

Ask if anyone can explain what an earthquake is. Explain that earthquakes occur when movement deep within the Earth causes movement of the outer layer, which is called the crust.

When pieces of the crust move, they release energy. This causes tremors, which can have a devastating effect on the earth's surface and the people who live where the earthquake occurs.

Tell students that the Earth is made up of many large plates. It is the shifting of these plates that can cause earthquakes. The San Andreas Fault in California is one of the places in the world where one may see the effects of two plates moving against one another.

Volcanoes

Have a class discussion about volcanoes. Explain that under the Earth's crust is the layer of mantle, some of which is melted. The melted parts are called magma. Magma flows beneath the crust. Where magma breaks through weak spots in the crust, volcanoes form. When volcanoes erupt, they emit mostly lava, but some send up rock, ash, and gas, too.

One type of volcano is called a hot-spot volcano. A hot-spot volcano occurs when magma melts holes in the crust and rises to the surface. A rift volcano is one where crustal plates split apart and magma rises through the cracks. Another type of volcano is a sub-duction volcano. This type of volcano occurs when plates collide, one plate slips below another, and the magma melts the lower plate and gets through weak spots in the upper plate.

Drought

Tell the class that when a region receives much less rain than normal, it usually means drought for the area. Without rain, grass and crops cannot grow. People and animals have nothing to eat or drink. The region's water supply dwindles. Sometimes, if the drought is severe, it can destroy the land.

If the people in drought-stricken areas have no reserves or money to import food and water, they may die. Where lakes or rivers once were, a dry and cracked wasteland may be all that is left. It sometimes takes years for an area to become fertile again.

Try this experiment with the class to observe some of the effects of water on an area. Layer a shirt box top with a sheet of plastic wrap, then cover it with a few inches of soil. Repeat with two more box tops. Write a number from one to three on each box. Plant some fast-growing seeds, such as lima beans or sprouts, in the first and second boxes. Water each as needed and observe the growth of both boxes.

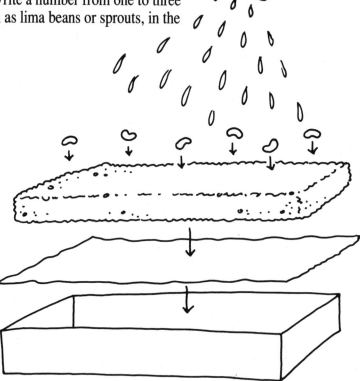

After the plants have begun growing, stop watering the plants in the first box. Observe the effect that a lack of water has on the soil and plants. (The plants wither and die; the soil becomes hard and cracked.) When rain does come to an area, what might be the difference between one with growing plants and one with no vegetation?

Next, tip the second and third boxes slightly (approximately a 20° angle). Using a watering can, sprinkle "rain" on the top edge of the soil. Compare what happens when the soil becomes saturated in each case. (The soil holds better in the planted box because of the root system holding it together; the soil runs down the slope in the box with no plant life growing in it.) Then ask volunteers to tell what might be the implications for populated areas near unplanted slopes during heavy rains.

Glaciers

Glaciers are enormous bodies of ice. They form in extremely cold places. The snow in the area turns to ice. Over hundreds of years, the ice grows larger and larger. Gravity pulls the glacier down to the lowest spot.

Most glaciers move only about 2 feet or less a day. Glaciers have created most of the earth's surface—lakes, mountains, and valleys. Crevasses in a glacier form when different parts of the glacier move along at different speeds.

Greenhouse Effect

MATERIALS:

2- or 3-liter plastic soda bottle
scissors
soil and small pebbles
fast-growing seeds
small lamp
2 thermometers

DIRECTIONS:

1. Wash out a 2- or 3-liter plastic soda bottle and let it dry. Then cut the bottle in half, as shown.

2. In the lower half, place a few inches of soil mixed with some pebbles. Plant some fast-growing seeds in the soil.

3. Fit the edge of the bottom half of the bottle inside the top half as shown, and stand the bottle on a flat surface. The inside of the bottle represents the air on Earth. The bottle represents Earth's atmosphere as it is affected by gases from things we use and activities we do. Normally, the atmosphere allows heat from the sun to pass through to the ground and prevents some from escaping back into space.

4. Explain to the class that Earth needs the atmosphere to hold in heat. Without it, the planet would be cold and no life could be sustained. However, the atmosphere has been changing. Some of the things people use and the activities people do produce gases that have been causing the change. These gases prevent heat from escaping our atmosphere. If the heat cannot escape, the temperature of the earth rises. Rising temperatures may cause ice near the North and South poles to melt, raising the water level of oceans. This could cause flooding and permanent resculpting of Earth: where there was once land, there might be sea; some places might become too hot to live in; some crops might not grow in the higher temperatures, possibly causing a shortage of food; animals might become extinct because they cannot live in the warmer climate.

5. Place a small lamp near the bottle, shining down into it. Let stand for a few hours. Tell the class that the lamp represents the sun and the heat it provides Earth.

6. Turn off the lamp. Remove the top of the soda bottle and suspend one of the thermometers down into it. Hold the other thermometer outside the bottle. Do not touch the bottom of the thermometers. Record the temperatures and compare the difference. The temperature of the air inside the bottle will be higher than the air outside. Tell children that this is called the **greenhouse effect**.

7. Have students research areas near ocean coasts that would be likely to be affected by flooding. Find out the names of some animals that thrive in cooler climates and might not be able to function in warmer temperatures. Discover which types of food grow in cooler areas and might die out if temperatures become warmer.

Cloud Investigations

Discuss with the class the three basic types of clouds: puffy cumulus clouds, layered stratus clouds, and feathery cirrus clouds.

Cirrus clouds, including cirrocumulus and cirrostratus clouds, form high in the sky, usually above 16,500 feet. They are always made of ice crystals and are capable of producing a halo effect around the sun or moon because of the refraction of the light shining through the ice crystals.

Clouds found at middle heights, from about 6,500 to 23,000 feet, include altocumulus and altostratus. These clouds are made of water droplets, ice crystals, or both, and have varied densities. (Visibility inside them may be anywhere from only a few feet up to a mile.)

Low clouds include fog and stratus, stratocumulus, cumulus, and cumulonimbus clouds. The height for these clouds ranges from Earth's surface to about 6,500 feet. These clouds are made entirely of water droplets and are usually very dense.

The cumulonimbus is in a category by itself. This type of cloud is capable of forming at any level in the sky and producing nearly all the other cloud types. It is this type of cloud that usually brings rain, and sometimes sudden thunderstorms.

If desired, borrow books containing information about different types of clouds from the school library. Observe the pictures of each type. Take the class outside with paper and pencils to study clouds. Ask students to write descriptions of the clouds that are viewed, and try to guess the names of these clouds.

Back in the classroom, look through the books to identify the clouds that were seen and check on the guesses made outside.

Reproduce the art on page 17 three times for each student. Distribute blank calendars to the class. Each day for a month, have students go outside and observe the types of clouds they see in the sky. Have each student glue into the square a picture of the clouds that most closely resemble those observed that day. Ask them to note also what kind of weather there is that day.

If desired, create a worksheet using a partial calendar with pictures of different clouds in each day. Ask questions based on the calendar, such as:

Predict the weather that might accompany these cloud formations.

What types of clothing might you wear when you observe these clouds in the sky early in the morning?

Identify three kinds of clouds shown on the calendar.

Each day, have students bring in the weather section from their local newspaper. Compare how different newspapers present the weather, from very basic to more sophisticated information. Discover any patterns in the various areas on the weather maps occurring during the week (for example, steady or shifting temperatures; consistent or changing cloud cover; and continuing rain or sun). Ask students to predict the type of weather for the next day before they gather the next weather map. Or have them predict what the next week's weather might be like based on the current week's weather.

Cloud Investigations

Weather Station

MATERIALS:

thermometer
camera and film
weather vane
barometer
rain gauge
wind gauge
record book and pencil

DIRECTIONS:

1. Place a thermometer in a shaded and well-ventilated area, such as on a wall under an overhang, so direct sunlight does not hit it. Choose how many times during the day to take the temperature (perhaps once early in the morning, once in the middle of the day, and once before school lets out). Ask students to compare the temperature readings with those of television and radio meteorologists and the newspaper weather page.

2. Use a camera to take pictures of the different types of weather observed. Different cloud formation photographs can be compared to those found in books, then identified and labeled. Various types of weather conditions may be photographed and labeled as well.

If desired, photograph the sky at different times of the day and evening to help children study light, dark, shadows, and clouds.

3. Show students a **weather vane** and ask if anyone knows how it is used. Explain how a weather vane shows from which direction the wind is blowing. (For example, if the pointer is aiming north, then the wind is coming from the north.) If desired, you may wish to have students construct simple weather vanes by cutting some sort of shape from construction paper and backing it with oaktag. (Traditional designs for vanes include the rooster and an arrowhead.)

4. When mounting the shape onto oaktag, have each child glue around the edges and inner space, leaving a 1" opening along the middle of the bottom edge and halfway up to the closed top. Stick an unsharpened pencil into the opening. Then mark North, South, East, and West on the pencil. Ask children to choose various times of the day for recording the direction of the wind.

5. Tell the class that a barometer is useful in checking the air pressure. Low pressure indicates storms; higher pressure indicates good weather. If you know a storm is approaching, take readings frequently to discover how fast the pressure is dropping, and how far.

6. **Rain gauges** are useful to find out how much rain has fallen during a storm or rainfall. A measuring cylinder with a funnel attached to the top and left out in an open space will catch water falling. Make sure the rain gauge is placed securely on level ground. After the rain has stopped, or at intervals during the rain, take a reading. Remember to empty it before recording the next day's rainfall.

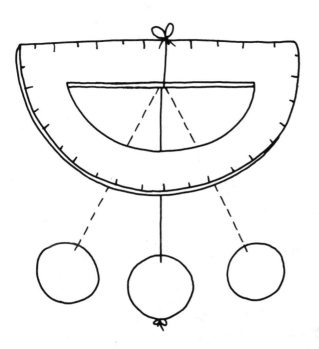

7. A **wind gauge** will tell you how fast the winds are blowing. To make one, hold a protractor upside down so the curved side is facing down. Tie a light ball, such as a Ping-Pong ball, to the upper edge of the protractor so it hangs below the curved edge. (The line used to tie the ball to the protractor must be in the center.) To check it, hold the protractor so the line falls along the 90° marking. As the wind blows, the ball will move. Record how many markings the line crosses before it heads back to the center marking.

8. Use a class record book for writing down all data collected during these studies of the weather. Try to include a photograph taken each day to illustrate the weather conditions. Have class discussions about comparing and contrasting the days' recordings. Ask volunteers to try to predict what recordings will be like in other seasons.

What's That Hole?

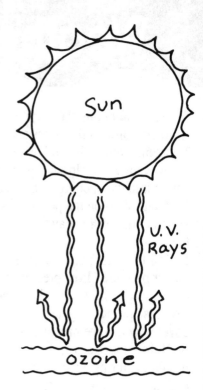

Tell students that **ozone** is a gas existing in our atmosphere, about 15 to 30 miles above Earth. Ozone protects us from dangerous ultraviolet light from the sun. (Some ultraviolet light is okay, but too much would be disastrous.) Without the ozone, the sun would burn us and stop many things from growing.

Scientists discovered the first hole in the ozone over Antarctica. This hole is currently about the size of the United States. Later, another hole was discovered over the Arctic. Both these holes change in size and shape as the seasons change. However, they signal a huge problem for the environment.

Ask if anyone knows some of the things that can cause depletion of the ozone layer. Explain that the main cause of this problem is the use of chemicals called chlorofluorocarbons (CFCs). These chemicals may be found in plastics (computers, TV sets, radios), foam packaging, air conditioner and refrigerator coolants, furniture cushions, and jewelry.

Elicit suggestions from the class about things that can be done to help stop the depletion of the ozone layer. Suggest that one thing people can do is to boycott products containing CFCs. We can write to manufacturers and ask our politicians to create laws, or strengthen existing ones, meant to reduce, if not stop altogether, the use of CFCs in products. Another strategy is to make flyers or short newsletters about the environment to inform others about what can be done to prevent further abuse of the ozone layer.

Ask each student to create a poster or a newsletter about the ozone layer. Children may wish to draw or cut pictures from magazines showing people misusing products containing CFCs. For example, a student may show a person standing in front of a refrigerator looking at what's inside as he or she takes time to choose what to take out (the refrigerator must work harder to make up for all the cold leaving while the door is open). Another poster might depict new packaging for eggs and other products. Encourage children to add pictures of activities that do not affect the ozone layer, such as gardening or riding a bicycle in a park.

Ask each student to title his or her poster or newsletter. Place the posters and newsletters on a bulletin board under the heading "Ozone Alert!"

Rock Collection

Rocks are everywhere. They make up mountains, they are hidden under soil and oceans, or they project out of the soil. Ask if anyone knows what rocks are made up of. (Minerals.) Tell students that a rock may be made of just one mineral or, like many rocks, a combination of them. Rocks tell us what the Earth was like long ago.

All rocks are divided into three main groups. One group is called **igneous** rocks. When liquid minerals are squeezed up near the Earth's surface, they cool slowly over a long period of time. The cooled rock becomes solid. Another way igneous rock forms is when hot igneous rock, which comes from volcanoes and is called lava, cools and makes solid igneous rock. One example of igneous rock is granite.

Another group is called **sedimentary** rocks. Air, rain, and wind cause rocks to change in a process known as **weathering**. The rocks are broken into pieces that the wind and water carry away. As they are carried, the rocks are broken into smaller pieces and eventually may be dropped into the ocean. These small rocks may become part of a beach or settle to the bottom of the ocean in a layer. Gradually, more layers form on top of old ones. The pressure of the top layers on the bottom layers packs them into rock. Different minerals are carried by water into the spaces in these new rocks and cement the loose rock into solid rock.

Shells from dead animals also fall to the sea bottom. The shells are made of a mineral called lime, which mixes with other minerals in the sediment to form other kinds of sedimentary rock. Examples of these rocks are sandstone, limestone, and shale.

The third group of rocks is called **metamorphic** rocks. All metamorphic rocks were once igneous or sedimentary rocks. When rock is heated or pressed together for a long time, it can change. Each type of rock will change into a certain metamorphic rock. For example, granite turns into gneiss, sandstone turns to quartzite, and limestone turns to marble.

Ask students to collect rocks from different places over a specified period of time. A good place to find rocks is construction sites. (Emphasize to students that they should first obtain permission from a site foreman who will vouch for their safety.) There, one can find many different rocks that have been displaced from the soil.

If a student is going on vacation, ask him or her to try to bring back some rocks. Compare rocks taken from the city with those found in the mountains and with those from the seaside. Are there similar properties common to all of them? What are the differences? Have students try to categorize the rocks into one of the three groups: igneous, sedimentary, or metamorphic.

To help students learn more about the properties of rocks, place a rock in a plastic bag and close it securely. Use a hammer to tap the rock and break it apart. Repeat on other rocks, and have children compare and contrast the insides of these rocks. What minerals can be found? How are the outsides compared to the insides?

Encourage students to research the rocks they have collected and try to find pictures of them in books borrowed from the library. If desired, have children make labels to identify the rocks. Then mix up the labels and see who can match all the labels to the correct rocks.

Versatile Water

It's wet!

There are many properties of water with which students will be familiar. Divide the class into small groups to perform some experiments that will show some different properties of water.

Begin by placing containers of water on each table. Ask each group to take a few minutes to write down as many properties of water as they can. Then have the groups share their thoughts with the class, and record students' comments on the chalkboard. Some properties include:

Water is made of hydrogen and oxygen.

It can be found in three phases—liquid, solid, and gas.

Water takes the shape of its container.

Water expands when cold and contracts when hot.

It is capable of changing things, such as the bends in a river or the rock under a waterfall.

Have each group perform a discovery activity about the cohesive ability of water. For each group fill a cup with a saucer under it completely to the top with water. Notice the smooth skin of the water. To test how strong the skin is (how cohesive the water molecules are), try this activity. Drop a penny into the cup. Did it overflow? Keep putting pennies into the cup, one at a time. As more pennies are added, notice how the skin shivers but does not break. This is because the cohesive ability of the water molecules is very great. Ask students to compare how many pennies it took before water spilled over the rim of the cup of each group.

Water can erode soil and weather rock. Create a dirt pile and measure its height and width on a chart. Fill a watering can with water and sprinkle some onto the top of the pile. Observe the streams that form and wash away dirt. Draw the dimensions of the new pile. Ask students what they think might happen if a heavy rainfall occurred over hillsides covered only with soil. What do they think might happen if there were trees and other plants rooted in the soil?

Versatile Water

Another experiment will help students observe the weathering capability of water. When water causes rocks to hit and rub against one another (as in streams in which water runs over rocks), and when water swirls with sand and rocks, the force of the water wears down the rocks' surfaces. Collect some sharp-edged pebbles and place in a jar. Fill the jar halfway with water. Ask students to predict what they think will happen to the pebbles. Take turns shaking the jar; it must be shaken many times.

As students take turns shaking, ask them to remember how many times they shook the jar. Have them write down their total on a chart. Every 200 shakes, take a look at the pebbles. Have they changed in any way? Continue shaking until a change in the shape of the rocks occurs. Then have students shake the jar more to see how the pebbles might change further.

Sum up the discussion by showing the importance of clean water in nature. Point out that water is a vital part of plant and animal (including human) lives. Many animals depend on water for a home, for drinking, and for spawning. Without water, plant life would die. Without plants, animals (including humans) would die. The human body is approximately two-thirds water. Humans cannot go longer than approximately 48 hours without water. Explain to the class that when water becomes polluted, the supply is depleted not only for humans, but also for plants and for other animals.

Here is a simple activity for observing how polluted water can affect plant life, and eventually, animal life. Cut the ends off two stalks of celery. Place one in a cup of clean water. In a second cup of water, drip 10 drops of blue food coloring. Place the other stalk in this cup. After about one hour, ask students to observe the stalks. What happened to the stalk in clear water? The stalk in the colored water? Tell the class that just as the coloring got into the stalk, so can pollutants enter a water supply and nearby plants. What might happen if animals ate these polluted plants? What might happen if people ate animals or plants that are polluted?

Oil and Water Don't Mix

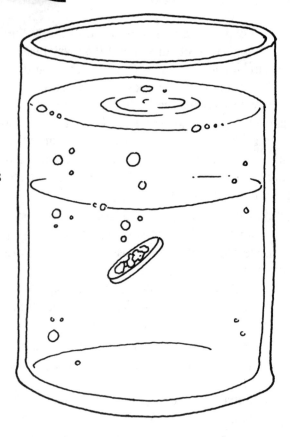

MATERIALS:

> vegetable oil
> corn syrup
> rubbing alcohol
> water
> food coloring
> clear plastic containers with caps
> newsprint and colored markers
> paper clips, pennies, buttons, small pebbles, feathers

DIRECTIONS:

1. Divide the class into small groups. Distribute all five liquids, containers, and test materials to each group.

2. Instruct one student in each group to fill a clear plastic container halfway with oil. Have the student mix food coloring with water and continue filling the container to the top.

3. Ask students to observe how the oil sits on top of the water. What do they think might happen if they shake the containers? Encourage students to describe what they see (water and oil mixed, oil coming to the top, water settling to the bottom, air bubbles forming).

4. Have another student in each group fill a container halfway with corn syrup and halfway with water mixed with drops of food coloring. Observe what happens when the containers are held still and when they are shaken. Repeat these observations using different combinations of the liquids. Have each group make a chart on newsprint showing the results of each of their mixtures.

5. Now test the viscosity of the liquids. Fill each container 3/4 full with a different liquid. Let each student take one paper clip and hold it the same distance above his or her container. On the count of three, tell everyone to drop the paper clip into the container and count how long it takes for the clip to settle to the bottom. Repeat using the other test materials (except feathers).

6. Ask each group to create another chart to show the conclusions of these tests. Which liquid is the most viscous? The least viscous?

7. A final experiment will demonstrate to students the seriousness of oil spills on water sources and animal life. Fill one container halfway with oil, and another with water. Drop some feathers in both containers. Wait a minute, then take the feathers out. What happened to the feathers in each liquid? After drying them for a minute, observe how the oil left the feathers matted. What are the implications for birds who get caught in an oil spill? (The oil may get under their feathers and weigh them down until they drown, or it may ruin their feathers and leave them with no insulation in the cold ocean waters, freezing them to death.)

8. Tell the class that oil is also difficult to clean. It may spread, destroying plants and animals as it goes, and it may form tarballs. The tide might bring it out to the ocean or carry it to shores. Some oils sink and some float. The oil has effects students may not think of. For example, birds that survive oil that has polluted the water may make it to shore, then poison themselves when they try to clean their feathers. Bald eagles eat some of these birds. When this happens, the food chain continues to be polluted, hurting animals and plant life.

Water Seepage

MATERIALS:

white sand
water
small baking pan
food coloring
vinegar
baking soda

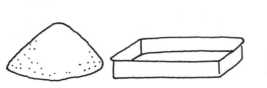

DIRECTIONS:

1. Have a class discussion about water pollution. While we all recognize that dumping pollutants into rivers, lakes, and oceans is harmful, emphasize to students that putting polluting materials in the ground can also be very dangerous. To illustrate how, try the following experiment:

2. Wet some white sand and put it in a small baking pan. Make two separate indentations in the sand, approximately 1 1/2" apart. Place a small amount of water in each hole.

3. Put a few drops of food coloring in one of the holes. Ask students to describe what happens.

4. Repeat the experiment, substituting 1-2 tablespoons of vinegar in one hole and 1-2 tablespoons of baking soda in the other. What happens?

5. Ask students to imagine that one hole is a freshwater well from which you get water, and that the other hole is a garbage dump. What problems could occur? What if the garbage dump contained toxic waste?

6. Try repeating the experiment with the two holes separated by different distances. Ask students how distance affects the amount of time it takes to contaminate the "clean" water.

7. Brainstorm about the things a land-use planner must take into account in order to drill freshwater wells. Write children's comments on a large piece of oaktag. On another piece of oaktag, write down the things a planner must think of when building a landfill for garbage. On a third piece of oaktag, write down students' comments about what things must be considered when building homes near a lake. Attach the oaktag posters to a bulletin board under the title "Things to Think About."

25

What Can Go Wrong?

Name _____

There are many sources of water pollution. Look at the illustration below. Identify the different types of pollution likely to come from each source.

1. _____
2. _____
3. _____
4. _____
5. _____
6. _____

Some sources of pollution may contribute more than others. Can you think of any solutions to the problems above? _____

_____

_____

A Drop of Water

Name _____

Look at the picture below. Use a blue pen to draw arrows showing the path you might expect a drop of water to follow.

At what points do you think pollution might cause problems with the water supply? Remember to consider air pollution as well as water pollution. Use a red pen to indicate where the water cycle might become polluted.

Water Consumption

Divide the class into groups of three. Give each group a sheet of newsprint and a different-colored marker for each member. Ask students to brainstorm on all the ways people use water.

When each group is finished, ask students to circle four ways we most frequently use water. Have a member of each group identify the four they picked and explain why those were chosen.

Write the four answers from each group on the chalkboard. Decide with the class which uses are necessary to our survival and which are secondary. Circle those uses that are necessary and have the class explain why those uses are so important to people. Then have the students tell why, although some uses are not vital for our survival, they are important to people.

Discuss with the class the following facts:

> The Earth's surface is over 70% water. The fresh water that people use comes from just 1% of it.

> Our fresh water comes from streams, rivers, lakes, and underground.

> More than 90% of the world's drinkable water comes from underground. The water running underground carries with it everything it passes through. Rainwater and melted snow that seeps into the groundwater carries with it gasoline, oil, pesticides, and other matter it has washed over.

> A person can live for weeks without food, but only a few days without water.

> The average person uses about 168 gallons of water a day. Just one flush of the toilet uses 3 1/2 to 7 gallons of water. A ten-minute shower uses 25 to 50 gallons of water. Leaving the water running while brushing your teeth could use up to 2 gallons of water. The National Oceanic and Atmospheric Administration predicts there might be shortages of available water in the 1990s.

Next, give each group fresh newsprint and colored markers. Ask the groups to come up with ways of saving water. After five minutes, ask each group to circle four of their best ideas. Then have them hang their papers around the classroom on the walls. Invite the groups to walk around the room reading other groups' suggestions. Then have students get back into groups and add three suggestions to their own papers that they saw and liked the best.

Have students create posters for the school bathrooms encouraging others to conserve water. You may also wish to have the class work together to write a newsletter with collected facts about water, water pollution, and water conservation. Send the newsletters to families and friends and encourage them to use some of the water-saving suggestions!

Air and Water Pressure

For this air pressure experiment, you will need a container filled with water, a clear cup, and a paper towel for each student.

Have each student crumple the paper towel and put it in the bottom of the clear cup. Explain to the class that they will be putting their cups into the container filled with water. Ask them to predict what will happen to the paper towel.

Tell children to turn the cups upside down and put them into the water. After a few seconds, take the cups out. Check students' predictions. Ask why they think the paper remained dry. (The air already in the cup kept the water from filling the space.)

Another experiment useful for observing the effects of air pressure requires a Ping-Pong ball and a 6" straw. Put the straw in your mouth and hold the ball above the straw. Begin blowing and gently release the ball. It will stay suspended in air above the straw as long as you continue blowing air through the straw.

Ask students for explanations. Inform them that the ball stays in the air stream because when air is in motion, its pressure is reduced. Therefore, the greater pressure of the air outside the stream forces the ball back into the stream whenever it begins to fall.

An experiment demonstrating water pressure will require a large can, a hammer, and a nail. At three spots, one above the other, hammer a hole into the can using the nail. Leave a 3" space between holes. Have a volunteer hold the can above a large tub or sink so everyone can observe the outcome of this experiment.

Inform students that the can will be filled to the top with water. Ask volunteers to predict what will happen. Fill the can to the top. Observe as the water comes from each hole in the can. The flow from the top hole is weak; the flow from the middle hole is a bit stronger; and the flow from the bottom hole is the strongest. Encourage the class to explain why the flows are so different. (The pressure of the water is greatest on the water at the bottom of the can and therefore it spurts out with the greatest force.)

Brainstorm with the class about how we use the pressure of air and water to help us. For example, windmills harness the forces of air to do work for us, and hydroelectric dams harness water power to produce electricity.

Ocean Life Mosaic

MATERIALS:

blue, green, and other colors of tissue paper
glue
sheets of newsprint or large piece of butcher paper
construction paper
crayons and markers
collage materials
scissors
tape

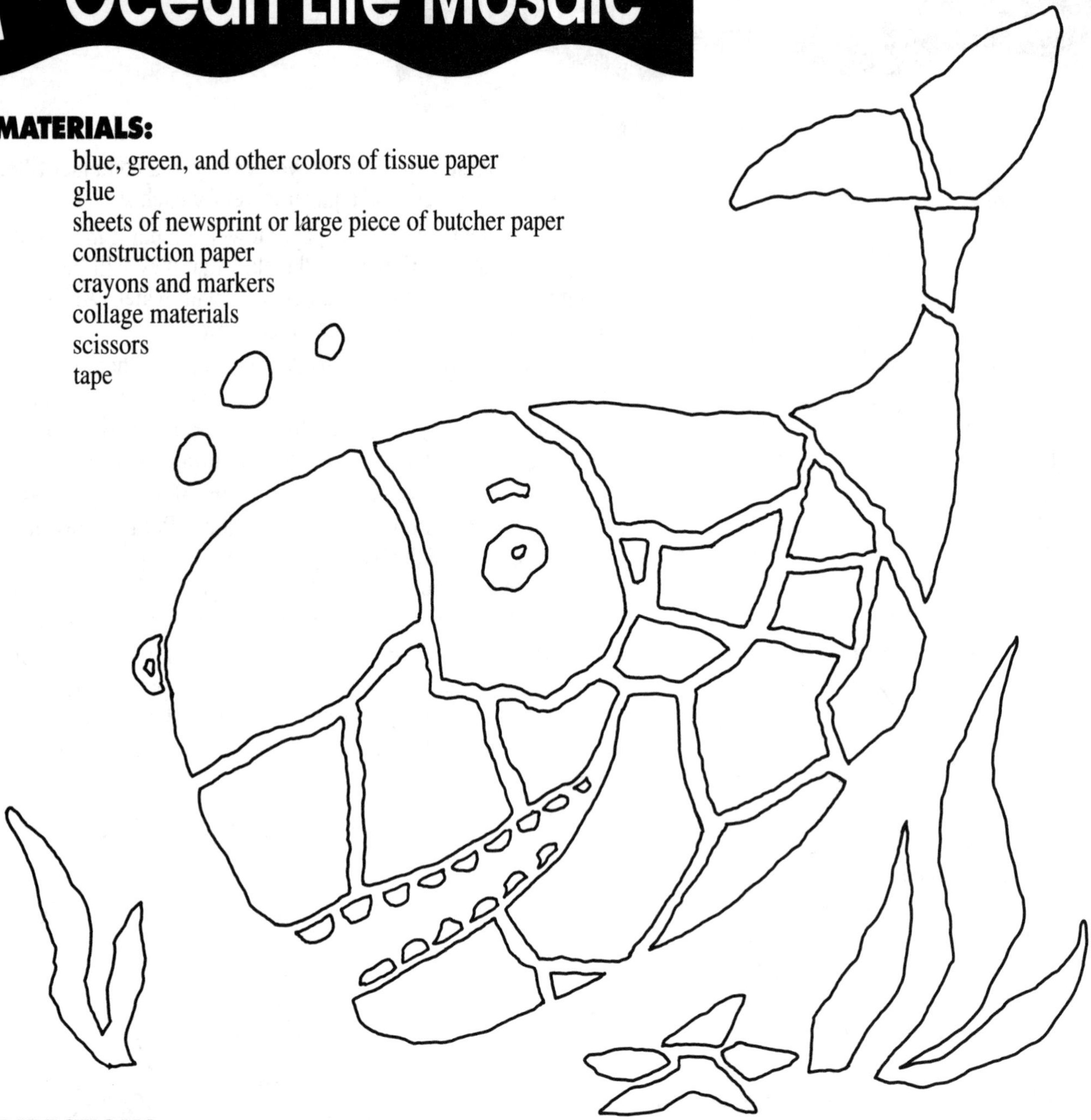

DIRECTIONS:

1. Divide the class into groups of four students each to make an ocean life mural. Assign a different task for each group, such as background, animal life, plant life, and labels. Each group must decide how to do its part of the mural. Display some pictures of mosaics so the class will get a sense of how they look.

2. Provide plenty of tissue paper, which may be torn in pieces and glued to the newsprint or butcher paper to form paper mosaics. Tape the sheets of newsprint together to form one large piece of paper before doing the background. The group should decide whether the water will be blue or green, or a mixture of the two.

3. The groups making the animals and plant life should use tissue paper, construction paper, and collage materials for their work. They may draw outlines of their animals or plants on construction paper, then tear or cut the tissue paper and glue it in pieces to the construction-paper outlines.

4. The label group may help out the other groups if necessary. This group should also be in charge of gluing the animals and plants to the background, then labeling the various animals and plants shown.

5. Display the mosaic in a hallway for all the school to enjoy.

30

Understanding Erosion

Create a large pile of dirt either outside or on a tarp on a flat surface indoors. Pack the dirt so it forms a solid hill.

Study the hill and write down any observations. Then sprinkle some water on the top of the hill. Study the effects of the water trickling down the hill. Did streams form? Did any of the streams come together to form rivers? Look at the bottom of the hill. Did any soil get washed down?

Repeat the sprinkling for a few minutes and observe what happens. What can the students infer from their observations about how streams and rivers form on Earth? Having observed the effects of erosion on a little hill in their experiment, what does the class think are the implications for people and the land on which they depend? Inform them that running water causes most of the erosion on the Earth's surface.

Brainstorm with students about what they think could be done to slow erosion of the soil. Discuss how the roots of plants help to hold soil in place. (See page 22 for a similar experiment.) Ask the students how erosion might affect the plants and animals who live in the area.

Tell students that years ago, farmers often accidentally destroyed the soil. They planted crops each year in all their fields, never letting the soil regain minerals and moisture. After repeated plantings, the soil could no longer support good crops. Then it became dry and unusable. When the wind swept across this land, topsoil just blew away. Today, farmers rotate the fields they use for their planting.

Deforestation is also a big problem. Explain to the class that people have been cutting down trees for many years without planting new trees in their places. Ask students what they think might happen if large areas of land were left empty. Encourage them to discuss the plight of animals that live in those trees and what happens to soil that is left bare. Can students think of ways to make sure that land is not left empty? What do they think will happen to the air if we keep cutting down trees without replacing them? (There will be more carbon dioxide in the air, and global warming would occur.)

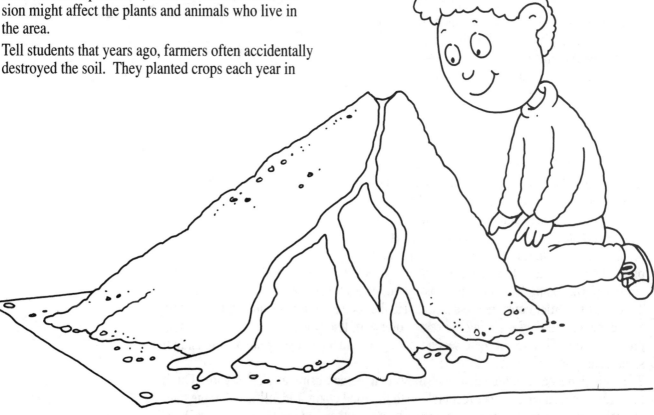

Food Web Mobile

MATERIALS:

crayons or markers   hangers
6" paper plates   straws
hole puncher   glue
different-colored yarn   paper

DIRECTIONS:

1. Ask if anyone can define a food chain. Explain to students that a food chain tells us how food energy is passed along from one organism to another. Green plants are producers and are the first in the chain. Next comes the animal that eats the plant—this is the first-order consumer. The animal that eats the first animal is the second-order consumer. (For example, a rabbit eats plants; then an owl eats the rabbit.)

2. Food chains often overlap with each other. The consumer of the rabbit might be a snake instead of an owl. A deer also eats plants, and a mountain lion or a person might eat the deer. A food web shows how food chains can be linked together.

3. To make a food web mobile, distribute crayons or markers and paper plates to the class. Have students draw pictures of producers, first-order consumers, and second-order consumers. (Make sure each student has some overlap of consumers.)

4. When all producer and consumer pictures are finished, punch a hole in the top and bottom of each plate.

5. Ask each child to map out the food web on a flat surface. Place the plants on the bottom, the first-order consumers in the middle, and the second-order consumers at the top. (Be sure all consumers are placed above the animals they eat.)

6. Have each child tie a 6" length of yarn from the plant plate to a straw. For each food chain connected to the plant plate, use a different-colored yarn. Using the apprpriate color yarn, tie each first-order plate to the straw. Tie each first-order consumer to a straw. Tie the second-order consumers to the straw above the animal they eat using the same color yarn that was used in the chain in the previous step. Tie each of these second-order consumers to a straw also, still using the same color yarn as before.

7. Lastly, have each student tie these straws to a hanger, using any color yarn. On the top straws, glue a small paper rectangle with the food chain it identifies. On the hanger, make a banner that reaches from one side to the other and entitle it "A Food Web."

Organism Classification

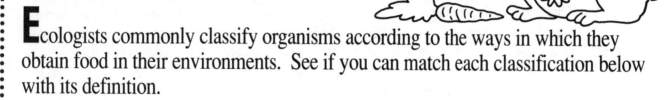

Name _____

Ecologists commonly classify organisms according to the ways in which they obtain food in their environments. See if you can match each classification below with its definition.

Classification	**Definition**
1. autotroph	**a.** consumes plants for food
2. heterotroph	**b.** consumes dead or decaying organisms
3. herbivore	**c.** manufactures its own food from carbon dioxide, water, light, and minerals
4. carnivore	**d.** feeds on dead organisms
5. omnivore	**e.** consumes animals for food
6. scavenger	**f.** feeds on living organisms
7. decomposer	**g.** obtains food from organic substances
8. parasite	**h.** eats plants and animals

Plant Responses

Divide the class into groups of three or four students each. Give a sheet of newsprint to each group and a different-colored marker to each member.

Ask the groups to brainstorm about the needs of plants. Each member of the group should write his or her idea using the color marker provided.

Ask one member of each group to mention three things plants need in order to survive. Discuss what might happen to plants if they did not receive the elements they need. What might the implications be for people?

Try this experiment about acid rain and its effect on plant life. Give each group two plants and give them the basics, that is, light, food, climate, and water. Each time the students water the plants, however, have them add some lemon juice to one plant's water supply. Be sure it is the same plant every time.

Have each group write down observations of its plants before beginning the experiment. As the weeks pass, tell the groups to write new observations on the appearances of the plants receiving the acidic water.

Explain that just as those plants are starting to die, so too do the plants, trees, and animals that are watered by rain containing acid. People may also be affected, directly and indirectly, from eating certain plants.

Have the class perform this activity to see what happens when the needs of a plant are changed. Plant lima beans in four different pots. Label them A, B, C, and D. Water each pot.

Place pot A in a dark cabinet, but water regularly. Place pot B in the dark and discontinue watering it. Place pots C and D in light, but only water pot D.

On a large experience chart, write down all the observations made as you wait for the plants to germinate. Then take all the pots from their places and compare and contrast. Discuss what might happen if the environment of certain plants was changed. What might be the results for people? (Plant loss, reduction of oxygen, increase in carbon dioxide, food loss, reduction in animals who depend on plant life for food.)

Food Factory

Name _____

Sunlight provides the primary source of energy on Earth. Human beings cannot turn sunlight into energy for their bodies—but plants can!

Most plants contain specialized structures called **chloroplasts**. The important part of the chloroplast is called **chlorophyll**. Chlorophyll absorbs the energy from sunlight and uses it to perform chemical reactions. These reactions convert carbon dioxide and water into sugar and oxygen.

This process of converting light into food is called **photosynthesis**. Label the different components of the photosynthesis reaction below.

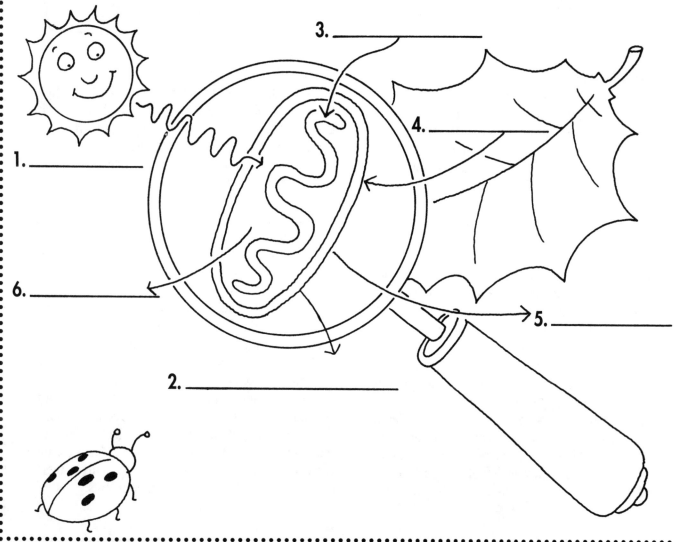

3. _____

4. _____

1. _____

6. _____

5. _____

2. _____

Animal Needs

MATERIALS:
- snails
- clear plastic containers
- black construction paper
- magnifiers
- apple, lemon, bread, cereal, carrots, cookie
- dirt
- water
- sandpaper
- small lamps

DIRECTIONS:
1. Collect snails from a nearby garden. (They may also be purchased from a biological supply house.)
2. Divide the class into groups of two and ask each group to make a home for their snails. Remind students of the habitat where the snails were found. Distribute the snails to the groups, trying to give each group at least two.
3. When all groups have made a home for their snails, ask them to explain why they used the materials they did for the home. Give each group a sheet of black construction paper. Ask the groups to take their snails from their homes and place them very gently on the paper. If the snails have closed over their shells, place them in a little puddle of water and see if they come out. If not, ask another group to lend one of its snails.
4. Have students observe the movements of the snails. Describe their bodies. Tell children to use magnifiers to get a good look at the two sets of antennae on each snail. Explain that one set is for smelling and feeling and that the longer set has eyes at the end for seeing.
5. Watch what happens when a finger is brought near the snails and when they are left alone. (Remind students that snails are living things and should be treated

as carefully as possible.)
6. While the snails are out, place various foods for them to sample. Observe which foods the snails eat or go near. Observe which foods they avoid. Make a chart noting their likes and dislikes.
7. This next experiment will help students in making sure their snail habitat is appropriately set up. Take the snails out of their homes and place them gently onto a sheet of sandpaper, near the edge. Do they like the feel of the rough paper? Now place them on the table. Do they like the smoothness of the table? How can students tell which they prefer? Spread some soil in a pan. Do the snails go over to the soil? Make half the soil damp and leave the other half dry. Which do they seem to prefer? Tell children to be patient. These observations may take minutes or an hour.
8. Another environmental test is to see if snails like light and heat or coolness and shade. Tell students to keep the snails in their homes. Over one-half of the container, tape a sheet of black construction paper. Shine a small light on the uncovered half. Which do the snails prefer? Ask the groups to explain how they came to their conclusions. Return the snails to their environments at the end of the experiments.

Endangered Animal Masks

MATERIALS:

newspaper
masking tape
wallpaper paste
water
mixing bowls
paints and paintbrushes
collage materials
glue

DIRECTIONS:

1. Have each student choose an animal that is endangered, one that is already extinct, or one that may become endangered soon (for example, Bengal tiger, elephant, spotted owl). Crumple a few sheets of newspaper into the shape of the head of the endangered animal. Hold its shape with a few small pieces of masking tape.

2. Show children how to create details on the face and head by crumpling smaller pieces of newspaper (for noses or eyes) or rolling them (for ridges or horns). Hold these in place with small pieces of tape as well.

3. When the head is complete, rip strips of newspaper. Make up bowls of wallpaper paste and water. Pour 2 cups of paste into each bowl and add water until the paste begins to thin. Have students dip fingers into the paste and coat the newspaper strips, then lay them onto the mask, as shown. Have them smooth each strip as it goes on.

4. Complete the first layer by facing the print in one direction. To do the second layer, face the print in the opposite direction, so students will know when a layer is completed.

5. When each mask is dry, paint it to resemble the real animal. Glue collage materials to the mask to make it more realistic (feathers, yarn for fur, beads for eyes).

6. Take out as much newspaper as possible from under the masks before displaying. Ask students to research how these animals became extinct or endangered, or why they might soon be. Encourage them to include facts about the animal, such as its preferred climate, where it can be found, food it likes, its habits, and any special characteristics it may have. Attach the writings near the masks on display. Invite the class to browse through. Then have other classes in to learn about endangered species.

Endangered Species Puzzle

6 down!

Name _____

Read each of the clues about endangered species below. Then fill in the answers to complete the crossword puzzle. Use an encyclopedia or a nature book if you need help!

Across
3. Has one or two horns
5. The fastest cat
9. The largest mammal of all (two words)
10. Large and strong ape
12. A powerful striped cat
13. A type of very large vulture

Down
1. A large wading bird
2. A spotted cat
4. Little fish that once stopped the construction of a dam (two words)
6. The largest land mammal
7. Majestic predator of the skies (two words)
8. A forest-dwelling cat with a gray or yellow coat
11. A flightless African bird

Bird Feeding Fun

Point out to students that when cold weather arrives, birds and other animals have a difficult time finding food. Have the class try to help the wild birds in your area by putting out food in a bird feeder.

Buy different types of birdseed, such as black-oil sunflower, red milo, and white millet. Set out 1/2 cup of each type of seed in close proximity to each other. Have students record the number of feeding visits and the different species that eat during a 30-minute period. (Place field guides about birds in the classroom reading or science center for students to use as reference.) At the end of each time period or day, measure the seed left in each cup. Repeat the test several times during the course of a week.

If desired, have students make a graph that shows the results of their birdseed study. Remind students that they should continue to put out food throughout the winter, since the birds will come to depend upon it.

Habitat Dioramas

MATERIALS:

crayons or markers
construction paper
oaktag
clay
collage materials
glue
large shoe boxes or shirt boxes

DIRECTIONS:

1. Borrow books from the library on the various biomes in the world. These include grasslands, desert, tropical rain forest, coniferous and deciduous forests, ocean, lake, and tundra. Discover which animals and plants thrive in each biome and in which type of habitat within the biome the animals make their homes.

2. Have each student choose a biome that interests him or her. Tell children to research the types of animals and plant life that live there. Students may wish to create animals and plants by drawing them on paper or oaktag and gluing appropriate collage materials to them to make them look more realistic. Or they may wish to use clay to sculpt the animals and plants for their particular habitats.

3. Before adding the animals and plants, encourage each student to make a background in his or her box resembling the chosen biome and habitat. Tell students to make sure to include the sky, the horizon, and the ground in each diorama. For instance, if the area is mountainous, a student would try to create the look of a high place. This can be done by drawing mountains in the background or by making a clay or paper mountain top on which to place the animals and plants.

4. Have each student write a short essay on the chosen biome, its plant life, and the animals and their habitats. Remind students to include how those particular animals and plants have adapted to their environments.

5. Place the dioramas around the room. Allow the class ten minutes to browse through the displays. When everyone has seen all the dioramas, ask for comments or questions from the group about what they have observed. If possible, find a visible display place to share the dioramas with the rest of the school.

40

Ecosystem Relationships

Name _____

Study the picture of this ecosystem. Then answer the questions below.

1. What kind of ecosystem is this? _____

2. Identify two food chains shown in the picture. _____
_____

3. In an ecosystem, living and nonliving things are interdependent. In the ecosystem above, what are two of the relationships between living and nonliving things? _____
_____

4. What might be three results of deforestation in this ecosystem? _____
_____

5. An ecosystem may be as small as a drop of water or as large as a planet. Identify two other types of ecosystems. _____
_____

6. Explain how you are dependent on the living and nonliving things in your ecosystem.
_____
_____

Micro-Ecosystems

Name _____

Within a particular geographic area, different ecosystems operate. These ecosystems may be made up of many smaller micro-ecosystems in which individual plants, animals, and microorganisms interact.

Look at each of the pictures below. On a separate piece of paper, write down the different relationships between the members of each micro-ecosystem.

Chemical Reactions

Name _____

Match each term of the science words below with its definition.

1. energy

2. electron

3. fusion

4. neutron

5. nuclear energy

6. proton

7. photon

8. matter

9. molecule

10. nuclear radiation

11. nuclear reaction

12. atomic number

13. atom

a. tiny, negatively charged particle revolving around the nucleus of an atom

b. combining of atomic nuclei to form a larger nuclei

c. particle in the nucleus of an atom that has no electric charge

d. ability to do work; the ability to set matter in motion

e. energy inside the nucleus of an atom that is released when the nucleus is split or fused with another nucleus

f. particle in the nucleus of an atom with a positive electric charge

g. substance of which physical objects are made up

h. tiny bundle of radiant energy that an atom may give off 1 at a time

i. very tiny units that make up an element of matter

j. event, sometimes accompanied by a release of energy, in which changes occur in the nuclei of atoms

k. energy given off by the nuclei of atoms in the form of waves or particles

l. number of protons in an atom

m. tiny particle of matter made up of 1 or more atoms

Element Construction

MATERIALS:

flour	measuring cups
salt	mixing bowls or containers
water	blue, green, and red food coloring
cups	toothpicks

DIRECTIONS:

1. Divide the class into small groups of three to four students each. Distribute flour, salt, cups, and three mixing bowls to each group. Instruct each group to mix 1 cup of flour with 1/2 cup of salt in each bowl.
2. Have each group add 10 drops of blue food coloring to a cup of water. Then have them add 10 drops of red food coloring to a second cup, and 10 drops of green food coloring to a third cup.
3. Mix enough blue water with the first flour-salt mixture to form a dough. (The dough should not be sticky; if it is, add more flour.) Repeat with the second and third mixtures.
4. Display the Periodic Table of Elements as students do this activity. Ask students to look up an element to model. For example, a group may choose carbon. That group would then find out the number of protons and neutrons in the nucleus of the carbon atom, which is six. The carbon atom also has six electrons whirling about the nucleus.

Carbon!

5. To make the carbon atom, the group would then make six small blue protons (ball-shaped), six smaller red neutrons, and six even smaller green electrons. The protons and neutrons may be stuck together, since they are found in the nucleus. The six electrons may be attached to the nucleus using toothpicks. (Remember to reinforce to students that the blue dough symbolizes protons, the red dough symbolizes neutrons, and the green dough symbolizes electrons.)
6. When the class is finished making their element atoms, ask them to go around the room looking at their classmates' work. Have them write down which element they think each group has made.
7. When everyone is seated, ask each group to identify its element. Students can check to see how many they guessed correctly.
8. This activity may also be done by making compounds, such as water (H_2O). A student may make this compound by using two blue balls of dough to represent the hydrogen and one red ball of dough to represent oxygen. The guessing activity may be repeated for identifying the compounds as well.

What's the Difference?

Name _____

Next to each item, write whether it is an element, a compound, or a mixture. Remember—an **element** is a substance that cannot be separated into simpler substances by chemical changes; a **compound** is composed of two or more elements, chemically united, and can be separated by a chemical change; a **mixture** is composed of two or more elements and/or compounds and can be separated by physical means.

1. gold _____

2. air _____

3. table salt _____

4. aluminum _____

5. water _____

6. carbon dioxide _____

7. soil _____

8. lead _____

9. copper sulfate _____

10. flour and salt _____

Simple Machines

Beep Zeep

Name _____

Machines are everywhere! Look at each picture below. Then write the name of each machine, and any combination of simple machines that make up each one, on the lines provided.

_____

_____

_____

_____

_____

_____

_____

Inclined Planes Experiments

MATERIALS:

1'-, 2'-, and 3'-long boards of wood
rectangular blocks
tennis balls
masking tape
rubber bands
paper clips
toy trucks
light-weight books

DIRECTIONS:

1. A good place to perform this experiment is in the gym. Begin by stacking four rectangular blocks in three separate piles of equal height, with approximately 1' between each pile. Lay one edge of a 1'-long board on the first pile, a 2'-long board on the second pile, and a 3'-long board on the third pile, all facing the same way. Make sure there is plenty of room in front of the boards.

2. Choose three students to stand behind the boards and hold one tennis ball each at the top of each incline. Ask volunteers to predict what will happen to the balls when they are released. Then ask if the length of the boards will have any effect on the outcome. See if students can estimate how far the ball from each inclined plane will roll.

3. Write students' comments on a chart. Then perform the experiments to see who guessed correctly.

4. Now test to find out if the height of an inclined plane has any effect on an object rolling down. Repeat the experiment using six blocks instead of four. Compare the results. Did the balls on the higher planes roll farther at each board length?

5. Next, try some experiments pulling objects up an inclined plane. Set one edge of a 3' board on a pile of four blocks. Set the other 3' board on a pile of eight blocks.

6. Open two paper clips so they form "S" hooks. On one end of each hook, attach a rubber band; hook the other ends to same-sized toy trucks. Position a truck at the bottom of each plane.

7. Choose two students to loop one finger into a rubber band and pull the trucks up the planes. Which plane is easier to pull something up—the one with the smaller angle or the larger angle? Repeat the experi-

ment, using different angles.

8. Try doing this experiment using light-weight books tied with string. Ask students to predict which would be easier to lift—something with wheels or something that will rub along the plane. Point out to the class that a good indication of how much energy is necessary for these two experiments is to watch how much the rubber bands stretch out while pulling the objects up the planes. The more the bands stretch, the more energy required; the less they stretch, the less energy required.

Lever Experiments

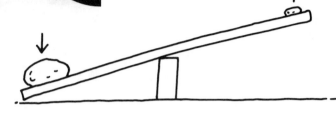

MATERIALS:
> yardstick
> block of wood
> large rock and a smaller rock
> yarn with paper clip attached to end
> scissors, hammer, pencil sharpener, doorknob

DIRECTIONS:
1. Tell the class that there are three parts to a lever: the **fulcrum**, the **effort arm**, and the **resistance arm**. The different types of levers depend upon where the basic parts are located.
2. Lay a yardstick on a wooden block, as shown. Observe how the longer end will go down to the floor. Now place a large rock on the shorter end of the stick. What happens? (The end with the rock goes down.)
3. Place the smaller rock on the longer end and watch as the smaller rock forces the larger one up. Ask students to guess why. Explain that the smaller rock is farther from the block of wood, which is acting as the fulcrum. The longer a lever is (the long end of the yardstick), the more you can lift.
4. Ask volunteers to try moving the fulcrum around under the yardstick. Try to balance the two rocks. Try to lift some heavy objects using the lever. Is it easier when the shorter or longer end is under the object?
5. To demonstrate another type of lever, make a fishing pole by tying a piece of yarn to one end of the yardstick. Attach a paper clip to the other end of the yarn. Hold the end with the clip with one hand and place the other hand about 1' along the rod. Keeping the hand closest to the body still, move the other hand slightly in an up-and-down motion. Observe how a small movement at one end makes a larger movement at the other end. Ask students to point out the fulcrum, the resistance, and the effort. (The fulcrum is the hand nearest the body, the resistance is the other end of the rod, and the effort is the other hand moving the yarn.)
6. Experiment with other objects, such as scissors, hammers, pencil sharpeners, doorknobs, and so on. For example, try cutting with scissors open slightly, and then wide open with the paper close to the screw. Or, try taking a nail from a board with the claw of a hammer. When you push down on the handle, the nail comes up. Without this lever, it would be very hard to remove nails. Ask students to try to figure out where the fulcrum is on each object.

uh oh!

Gears on the Go

MATERIALS:

corrugated cardboard
scissors
oaktag
large brass fasteners

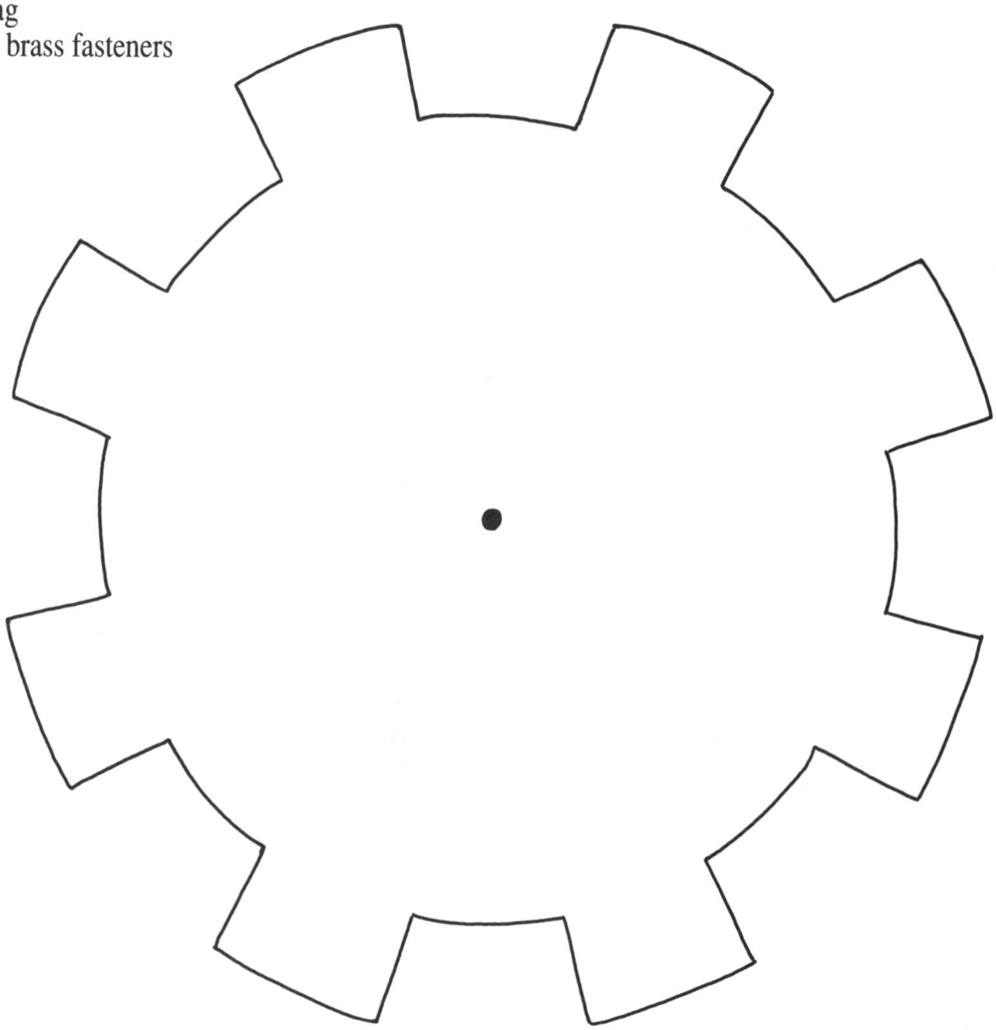

DIRECTIONS:

1. Reproduce the gear wheel pattern on this page. Trace it several times onto corrugated cardboard and cut out.
2. Cut a hole in the middle of each wheel. Attach one wheel to a piece of oaktag using a brass fastener. Attach the next wheel so the teeth of the first fit into the teeth of the second.
3. Before turning the first wheel, predict what will happen. Observe how the first wheel turns the next wheel in the opposite direction. Observe that the wheels turn at the same speed as well. Add more wheels, either in a straight line or in a different pattern, making sure the teeth of each pair of wheels line up with each other. Discuss the direction of each wheel.
4. Reproduce the wheel pattern again, this time reducing it if possible. Add this wheel to the oaktag and observe whether this wheel also goes in an opposite direction and whether it turns at the same speed as the larger wheels.
5. Allow students time to experiment with machines that use gears, such as a bicycle and an egg beater.

50

Energy Use

Name _____

Read Sarah's journal entry below. Then answer the questions about energy use.

January 16

7:00 a.m.—Woke to the sounds of the garbage collectors dragging the cans along the sidewalk and grinding the trash in the truck. What a pleasant way to wake up! Couldn't get out of my room because my little brother jammed the doorknob.

9:00 a.m.—Finally got to school. The toaster wasn't working, so I had to have some of my little brother's gross cereal. Then the hair dryer was broken, so I sat in front of the fan and tried to dry my hair that way. When I got to school, I was freezing. I chose a seat near the windows to get some sun and warm up.

12:00 p.m.—Jack, the cutest boy in my class, sat next to me at lunch! We talked about how cold it was outside, our classes, and whether or not we were going to the dance on Saturday night. He didn't ask me! I tried to get him to say who he was going with, but he was very secretive. I'll have to ask Jen to ask him tomorrow.

1:00 p.m.—Science class was really interesting today. We were comparing the growth of plants under different circumstances. The plants under the lights that we water are doing the best. The ones in the dark closet that we haven't watered are doing poorly. I'm going to take them home after the experiment and nurse them back to health. Ms. Price says I can take home a lamp for them. She's such a nice teacher!

3:00 p.m.—We went to the basketball game after school. We screamed so loud that our throats got sore. Between the sound of our screaming, the noise of the snowblowers outside, and the music from the band, I got such a headache! But I think our cheers helped the team win. And of course I screamed the loudest for Jack!

6:00 p.m.—We ate dinner. Dad microwaved some potatoes while Mom and I made a nice salad. Then we had some ice pops for dessert. Yum!

10:00 p.m.—Time for bed. I'm exhausted. Wait a second—I have to go tell my brother to turn down his radio. He plays it so loudly you can hear it across town. OK, I'm back. I have to remember to take the extra blankets out of the closet and put them by my bed in case it gets as cold as last night. I've got on my long johns, socks, a T-shirt, leggings, and two blankets already! I wish Mom would turn the heat up a little. Oh well, I'd better hit the sack. Bye!

Energy Use

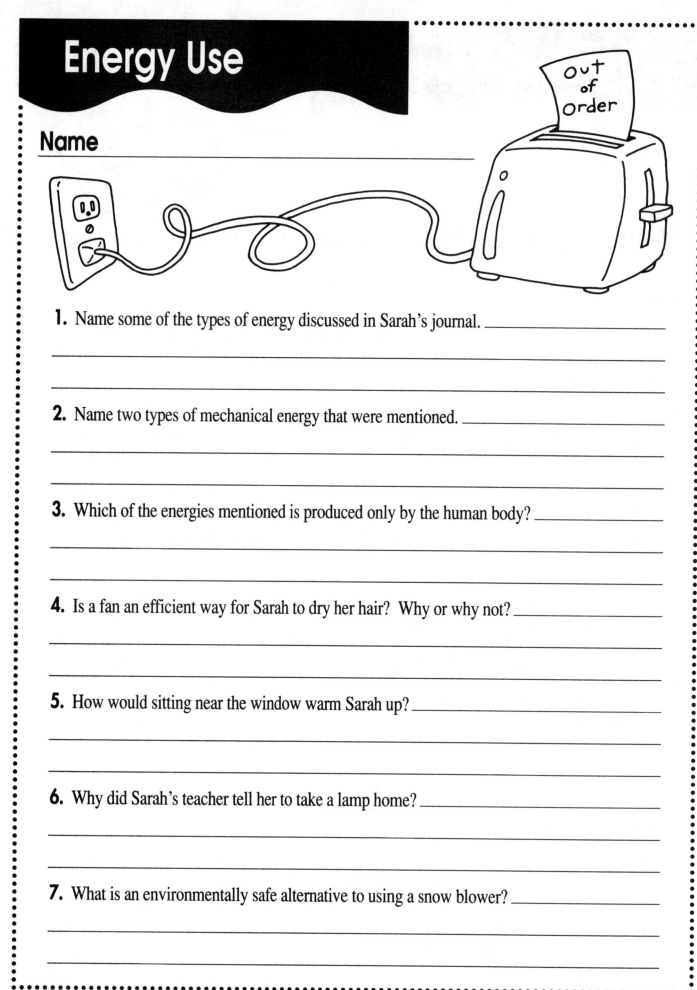

Name _____

1. Name some of the types of energy discussed in Sarah's journal. _____
_____
_____

2. Name two types of mechanical energy that were mentioned. _____
_____
_____

3. Which of the energies mentioned is produced only by the human body? _____
_____
_____

4. Is a fan an efficient way for Sarah to dry her hair? Why or why not? _____
_____
_____

5. How would sitting near the window warm Sarah up? _____
_____
_____

6. Why did Sarah's teacher tell her to take a lamp home? _____
_____
_____

7. What is an environmentally safe alternative to using a snow blower? _____
_____
_____

Appliance Energy Consumption

Name _____

Rank the appliances listed below according to how much energy you think they consume yearly. Write a 1 next to the appliance that you think uses the most energy and a 10 next to the appliance you think uses the least energy. Next to each appliance name, write one way in which you could help reduce its energy consumption. Make an "X" next to the appliances that perform jobs you could do yourself.

_____ room air conditioner _____

_____

_____ carving electric knife _____

_____

_____ dishwasher _____

_____

_____ microwave oven _____

_____

_____ radio _____

_____

_____ refrigerator/freezer (14 cubic feet) _____

_____

_____ color television (tube type) _____

_____

_____ electric toothbrush _____

_____

_____ vacuum cleaner _____

_____

_____ washing machine (automatic) _____

_____

Waste Not, Want Not

Name

Circle the energy "wasters" in the picture below.

What are some solutions to the problems you have circled?

_____

_____

_____

_____

_____

Heat Energy Experiments

To show the flow of heat energy, you will need two clear jars with equal-sized necks, food coloring, and a piece of cardboard.

Fill one jar with cold water and place a square of cardboard over the opening. Pour hot water into the second jar and mix in about 10 drops of food coloring. Make sure both jars are filled to the brim.

Holding the cardboard over the opening of the cold water jar, turn it over and place it on top of the hot water jar. Holding the necks of the two jars, carefully slide the cardboard from between the two. Ask students to predict what will happen. Observe as the hot water rises and the cold water sinks down. Explain to the class that heat energy flows from warmer objects or regions to cooler objects or regions. The warmer becomes cooler and the cooler becomes warmer until they are at the same temperature.

Here is an experiment to test which materials are good conductors and which are poor conductors of heat energy. Have volunteers hold both hands above a radiator for a few minutes. Take hands away from the radiator and put a wool glove on one hand, leaving the other hand uncovered. Which hand remains warm? (The one with the glove.) Since wool is a poor conductor of heat, the hand with the wool glove remains warmer longer.

Another test for conductors is to boil some water in an old can over a hot plate. When the water boils, turn off the heat. Place various materials (such as a spoon, thin block of wood, candle, straw, long twist of aluminum foil, rock, or shell) in the water one at a time, leaving a part of each exposed to air. After 30 seconds, touch the end that is standing up out of the water. Is it hot or cool?

Have a class discussion about uses of heat energy for people. How do we use heat and where are its sources?

Sound Energy Experiments

Explain to the class that sound is made when objects strike each other and rub against one another, or when an object is plucked or blown. The objects vibrate because of these actions, and it is the vibration that causes the sounds you hear.

Encourage students to create different sounds using their clothing, body, or objects in their bookbags. Try some experiments to discover the vibrations of objects. For example, stretch a rubber band and pluck it, watching the vibrations of the rubber band. Or strike a fork or tuning fork on a table and bring it to your ear, feeling the vibrations in your hand and hearing their sound.

Tell the class that sound travels through air in waves. Give pairs of students a rope to show how sound waves would look if they could see them. Ask two students to hold the rope at either end. Tell one student to shake his or her end up and down. Watch how the wave travels from his or her end to the partner's end. Then reverse the wave.

Explain to students that sound can also travel through many things, such as wood, string, steam pipes, or tubes. Ask students to listen to their heartbeats if they can. Then give them plastic tubing and funnels to create their own stethoscopes (or distribute play stethoscopes). Ask them to listen to their heartbeats with the stethoscopes. Tell them a stethoscope works because the sound travels through the air inside the tube.

Another activity for discovering how sound travels uses empty, round cereal boxes, such as oatmeal boxes. Divide the class into pairs of students and give each pair two cereal boxes. Instruct the groups to take the tops off both boxes and punch a hole in the bottom of each box. Then tie a toothpick to each end of a long, thin string. Stick the toothpicks in the holes at the bottom of the boxes and make sure they lie flat against the inside bottom of each box.

Ask the pairs to hold one box each and back up until the string is tight. Invite one student from each group to talk softly into the box. Students will observe that the vibrations from their voices pass to the bottom of their box, then to the string, then to the bottom of their partner's box, and into the air of their partner's box.

Discuss the fact that sounds can be high- or low-pitched. They may be soft or loud. Experiment with pitch by stretching different lengths and thicknesses of rubber bands across a sturdy, open container. What do the students observe? (The looser the band, the lower the pitch, and vice versa; the thicker the band, the lower the pitch, and vice versa; and the longer the band, the lower the pitch, and vice versa.)

Next, blow across the openings of different-sized bottles. What do students observe? (The larger the bottle, the lower the pitch; the smaller the bottle, the higher the pitch.)

Noise Pollution

Name _____

Circle the objects that contribute to the noise pollution in this house and the surrounding neighborhood.

What are some ways to reduce the noise pollution pictured here?

_____

_____

_____

_____

Electricity Investigations

MATERIALS:

- wool scraps
- balloons
- combs
- thread
- dry cells
- copper wire
- flashlight light bulbs
- tape (if bulb holders and screws on the dry cells are not available)

DIRECTIONS:

Explain to the students that static electricity is created when friction causes free electrons to leave an object and attach themselves to a new object, giving the new object a negative electric charge. When the new object is placed near an object with a positive charge, the two are attracted to each other (opposites attract). Static electricity works best on days that are cold and dry. Since water is such a good conductor of electricity, if the air is too humid, the charge will be too weak and the objects will not respond properly.

To demonstrate this concept, fill balloons with air. Place them next to a wall and let go. What happens? (The balloons fall.) Next, rub them with wool scraps and put them next to the wall again. Ask students to predict what will happen. (The balloons stick to the wall.) The friction of the wool with the balloons caused a transfer of electrons from the wool to the balloon.

Another good way to demonstrate static electricity is to hold one end of a 5" length of thread in one hand and a comb in the other. What might happen when the comb is brought near the thread? (Nothing.) What might happen if the comb is rubbed with the wool first? (The thread is attracted to the comb and will rise up to meet it.)

Rub Rub Rub Rub

An electric charge that is moving from one place to another is **current electricity**. The movement, or flow, of electrons from one place to another is called an **electric current**. To create an electric current, attach a wire from the negative terminal on a dry cell to the positive one.

Explain to the class that in order for the electric current to flow, a circuit must be formed. Electrons move from the negative to the positive in a circuit. Now try adding a light bulb and making it light. Remind students that in order for the circuit to work, the path of the electrons must take them from the dry cell and back to it again. Allow time for students to experiment with the materials.

When students have completed their circuits, ask them to describe the job of the wires. (They conduct electricity.) Encourage them to discover what other materials besides the wire would make good conductors of electricity.

Keeping the circuits set up as they are, remove one wire from each dry cell. Then cut the wire still connected to the dry cell and light bulb in the middle of the two. Connect the other wire back to the terminal.

Some suggested materials to try as conductors are rubber bands, crayons, forks, plastic knives, string, foil, and nails. To test which materials work as conductors, touch one at a time to the raw ends of the wire. If the light bulb lights, the circuit is complete and the material is a good conductor; if the light bulb does not light, the material is a good insulator.

Best Books About the Environment

1. *Understanding Ecology* by Elizabeth Billington (Frederick Warne, 1971)

2. *Going Green*: *A Kid's Handbook to Saving the Planet* by John Elkington, Julia Hailes, Douglas Hill, and Joel Makower (Puffin Books, 1990)

3. *50 Simple Things Kids Can Do to Save the Earth* by John Javana (Andrews & McMeel, 1990)

4. *Take Action*: *An Environmental Book for Kids* by Ann Love and Jane Drake (William Morrow and Co., 1993)

5. *Save the Earth*: *An Action Handbook for Kids* by Betty Miles (Alfred A. Knopf, 1991)

6. *SOS Planet Earth* series (*Water Squeeze*; *Power Failure*; *Nature in Danger*; *Air Scare*) by Mary O'Neill (Troll, 1991)

7. *Sierra Club Book of Our National Parks* by Donald Young (Little, 1990)

60

Continents Crossword

5 down.

Name _____

Figure out the answers to the clues below. Then write the answers in the appropriate boxes to complete the puzzle.

Across

3. The outer layer of Earth

4. One of Earth's largest land masses

8. The remains of plants and animals that lived a long time ago

9. An expert on the features of the Earth's surface

10. The energy that is released when pieces of the Earth's crust move

11. A "lost continent" that supposedly sank into the sea thousands of years ago

Down

1. An extension of a continent that slopes down into the ocean (two words)

2. The planet on which we live

5. A piece of land surrounded by water

6. A shaking of the ground thought to be caused by the movement of Earth's plates

7. A scientist who studies the Earth's insides

12. The vast continent thought to have once comprised all of Earth's land

Fossil Dig Game

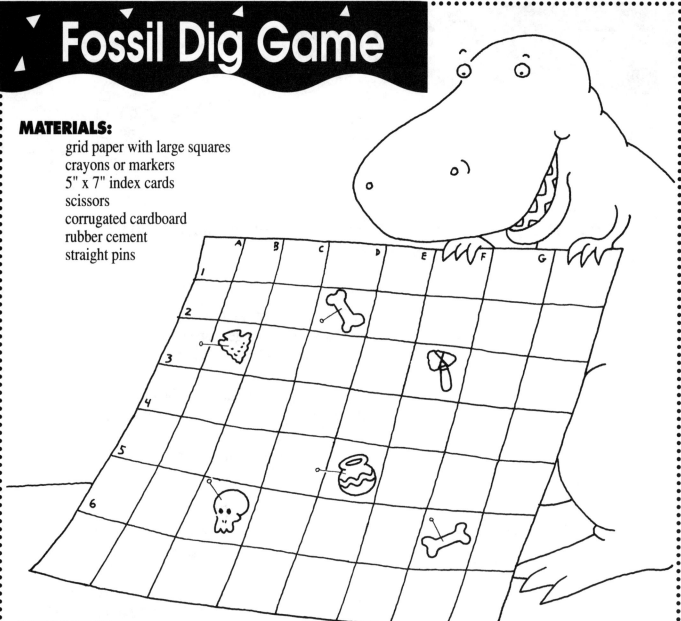

MATERIALS:

grid paper with large squares
crayons or markers
5" x 7" index cards
scissors
corrugated cardboard
rubber cement
straight pins

DIRECTIONS:

1. Lay out two large pieces of grid paper. Make small drawings on the index cards resembling things that might be found at a fossil dig, such as arrowheads, statues, pottery shards, and weapons. Be sure each drawing fits inside a square of the grid paper. Cut out shapes.

2. Attach a piece of grid paper to a piece of corrugated cardboard with rubber cement. Repeat. Over each box along the top of each grid, write a letter of the alphabet, beginning with A. Next to each box down the left side of each grid, write a number, beginning with 1. There should be two identical grids.

3. To set up the playing area, place the grids about 1' apart, with a barrier between them so players cannot see each other's boards. The barrier may be a stack of books or another board with supports to hold it upright.

4. Have each player randomly arrange the "fossils" on his or her playing grid. Give each player a small stack of straight pins to place in a pile next to his or her grid.

5. The youngest player goes first. Have that player call out two coordinates, such as "B5." The other player will insert a pin into the spot called on his or her grid. If the coordinates fall on a fossil, the player must call out, "Dig." The first player then calls out 2 more coordinates. If the coordinates fall on blank space, the player must call out, "Dirt," and the other player calls out two coordinates.

6. When all of one player's fossils have been pinned, that player is out of the game and the other player is the winner.

7. Store the boards and playing pieces in a pocket folder. Carefully place the pins in a small box before putting in a pocket.

62

Homes and the Environment

Ask the class to describe the environment in which they live. Do they live in the mountains, in the city, near water, in the desert, on the plains? What is the weather like? What types of animals and plants can be found nearby?

Discuss how the type of homes people have sometimes reflects the environment in which they live. For example, people in the desert sometimes live in one-story adobe homes. Adobe is a type of brick that helps keep the house cool in the hot summer sun. Since heat rises, most homes in the desert are just one story high.

Distribute paper and crayons or markers to the class. Have each student draw a picture of his or her home. Encourage students to describe how their homes fit into their environments. Ask them to explain how the things in their environment relate to each other. For example, if the students live in a city, they may mention that their form of transportation is the subway or bus. Since there are so many people, these are the easiest forms to take. Their homes may be in houses, like rowhouses or brownstones, or in large apartment complexes.

Borrow books from the library that have pictures and sections on places where people make their homes. Discuss how people adapt to their environments. In some coastal areas, people have homes on stilts. Others use boats on canals or rivers instead of cars to get around. Have students choose a place in which they would like to live someday. Encourage them to explain their choices and what types of home they would like to have.

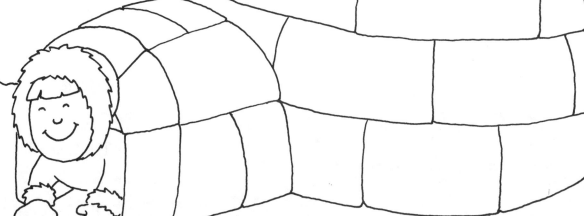

63

Transportation and the Environment

Name _____

Although certain forms of transportation, such as automobiles, can be found in many parts of the world, some areas are more likely than others to have a specific type of transportation. Match each form of transportation pictured to the area in which it is most likely to be found.

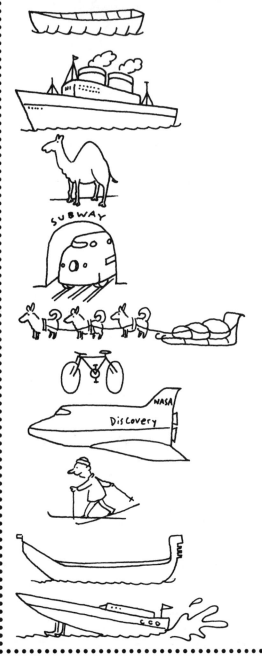

New York City

China

Moon

Sahara Desert

Venice, Italy

Norway

Inishmore, Aran Islands, Ireland

Everglades, Florida

The Yukon Territory

Atlantic Ocean

Environment Afternoon

Inform students that they will be holding an information fair for their parents and other classes. Ask the class to brainstorm on environmental issues, such as deforestation, erosion, water pollution, acid rain, and global warming.

Have students interested in a particular problem get together in a group. Try to limit each group to three or four students, maximum.

Allow time for groups to visit the library to research their topics. Groups may need to meet after school to plan how they will present their information. Encourage the groups to be creative. For example, they may dress in a costume or offer their information with a short play, a song, a poem, a conversation, a puppet show, a commercial, an advertisement for a product, an oral survey, something to eat that illustrates their topic (for example, the Earth Cake on page 11), a video, or a speech.

Tell groups to be prepared to hand out literature to interested visitors. They may type up their offerings on a typewriter or a computer and add pictures to their literature.

They should also create posters or murals for their section of the fair. They may use table space, floor space, and the walls for their displays. Encourage them to make up catchy phrases that people will remember.

Make sure groups provide their visitors with information on how to slow down the negative effects people are having on their environment. Remind students that their goal is to inform and persuade people to change some of their habits and help save our resources.

65

Recycled Paper

MATERIALS:

plain bathroom tissue
lint (from a clothes dryer)
warm water
small mixing bowl
small pieces of window screen
shallow pans
blotting paper or
    absorbent cloth
rolling pin

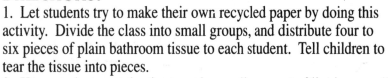

DIRECTIONS:

1. Let students try to make their own recycled paper by doing this activity. Divide the class into small groups, and distribute four to six pieces of plain bathroom tissue to each student. Tell children to tear the tissue into pieces.

2. Have students put the tissue and a small amount of lint in a small mixing bowl with about 1 1/2 cups of warm water. Stir the mixture until it has an even consistency. Tell students this is the pulp.

3. Place a small piece of window screen in the bottom of a shallow pan. Have students pour the pulp in and spread it out across the screen as evenly as possible.

4. Tell students to carefully lift each screen out of its pan. Have them place a piece of blotting paper or absorbent cloth over the screen.

5. Be sure each group holds this "sandwich" together carefully, then flips it over so the screen is on top. Use the rolling pin to squeeze out more water.

6. Lift off the blotter and the screen. Let the paper dry for approximately one day.

7. Let each group use their paper to write a message, draw a picture, or help make a class collage.

Renewable Resources

Name _____

Human beings use a great deal of energy every day. Most of the energy comes from nonrenewable sources, such as natural gas and petroleum. Some of the energy comes from plants, dams, windmills, and the sun. These are all renewable energy sources.

Find the energy words hidden in the puzzle below. The words may be written forward, backward, up, down, or diagonally. Circle each renewable energy source in blue pen. Circle each nonrenewable energy source in red pen.

```
D I E N E S O R E K
O K R L M L L T E M
N I O C N A L I P R
U S O I M W M D D A
C A P I K E U A O L
L O N A H T E L W O
N A T U R A L G A S
O S L O S I O I E L
R D I T M P R R O E
E A I D K E T M S S
T O N U C L E A R E
A I L U T A P T E I
W O O D N R A L K D
```

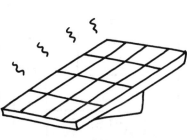

ethanol	nuclear	petroleum	solar	windmill
coal	natural gas	wood	animal	oil
kerosene	tidal	water	diesel	

Clean and Healthy Maze

Name _____

Find your way through the maze to a clean, healthy environment. Watch out for pollutants along the way!

What Would We Do Without It?

Name _____

Over time, people have become used to the convenience of certain disposable products, such as paper napkins and plates, cardboard boxes, and so on. Try to think of some reusable products that could be used instead of the disposable products listed below.

1. paper lunch bag _____

2. plastic grocery bag _____

3. cardboard packing boxes _____

4. paper cups _____

5. Styrofoam coffee cups _____

6. paper napkins _____

7. aluminum foil roasting pans _____

8. plastic wrap _____

9. disposable diapers _____

10. paper plates _____

Class Compost

DIRECTIONS:

1. Ask if anyone knows what a compost pile is. Explain that by using yard waste, such as grass clippings and leaves, one can produce a rich compost full of nutrients for flower and vegetable gardens.

2. Ask each child to bring in a small bag of waste materials appropriate for a compost pile, such as vegetable and fruit peelings, leaves, grass clippings, and weeds.

3. Outdoors, layer the leaves, grass clippings, and so on with some dirt. Add some water until the materials are moist, but not wet.

4. Leave the pile for a week or two, adding water occasionally if necessary to keep the pile moist. Then ask students to feel the outside of the pile. If composting is occurring, the pile should feel warm.

5. Continue observing the compost pile each week. Be sure to mix the pile occasionally with a pitchfork or a shovel to allow air contact and keep odors to a minimum.

6. Compost piles can stay warm through the winter months. Place a plastic sheet over the pile if necessary to keep it warm and moist.

7. After two months, have students observe the compost again. Have the materials changed? Encourage students to write about the differences they see. (The complete process should take approximately six months.)

8. When the composting cycle is complete, use the compost in the school flower garden.

Environmental Action Game

MATERIALS:

- crayons or markers
- scissors
- glue
- letter-sized file folder
- clear contact paper.
- playing pieces (e.g., coins)
- envelope
- oaktag

DIRECTIONS:

1. Reproduce the game board on pages 72-73 once. Color the game board, cut it out, and mount it on the inside of a letter-sized file folder.

2. Reproduce the game cards on page 74 four times. Mount them on oaktag, laminate, and cut apart. Place the cards in a pile on the game board.

3. Have each player choose a playing piece. (You may wish to have students use different coins, such as a penny, nickel, dime, and quarter, as playing pieces.)

4. Cut out steps 5 and 6, below. Glue them to the front of the file folder under the heading "How to Play."

5. The youngest player goes first. That player should draw a card from the pile and follow the directions indicated on the card. Then the next player goes.

6. Play progresses clockwise around the board. The first player to reach the Recycling Center is the winner.

7. Store the game cards and playing pieces in an envelope glued to the back of the file folder.

Environmental Action Game

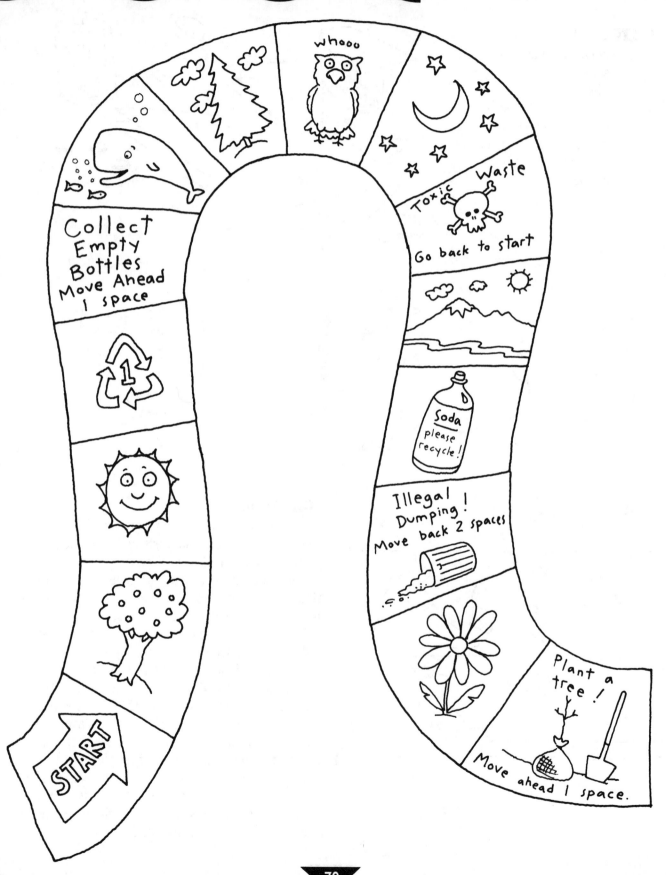

Environmental Action Game

Environmental Action Game

Sort It Out

Name _____

Recycling can help solve the problems our cities and towns have in disposing of solid waste. However, recycling only works if the materials are sorted properly.

Try to sort the materials below. Draw a circle in red around toxic waste, in blue around recyclable waste, in green around compostable waste, and in yellow around nonrecyclable garbage.

What Can You Save?

Name _____

Not only does recycling help to reduce the amount of solid waste a community produces, but the recycled materials themselves act as raw materials, which means fewer natural resources harvested for consumption.

In the space provided next to each drawing, describe what recyclable materials could replace the resource shown. Then tell what advantage you might expect from recycling this material.

Source	Alternate recycling source	Advantage of recycling
1.		
2. IRON ORE		
3. Sand		
4. crude OIL		
5. BAUXITE ORE		

Where Does It Go?

Name _____

For recycling to succeed, a particular industry must want to buy the recycled materials produced to use them as raw materials for a new product.

Can you think of some of the products that could be made using the following materials?

1. glass jars and bottles _____

_____

2. steel cans _____

_____

3. aluminum cans _____

_____

4. newspapers _____

_____

5. white paper _____

_____

6. plastic _____

_____

Plastic Problems

Have a class discussion about the different types of plastic. Explain to students that some plastics can be recycled, but others cannot. Six different "resins" make up most of the plastic products we use. Two of these resins, polyethylene terephthalate (PTE) and high density polyethylene (HDPE), are commonly recyclable.

Tell students that the most useful type of plastic is PTE, since manufacturers can make a variety of everyday products with this material.

Explain to the class that problems can arise when different kinds of plastics are mixed together. Since different plastics have different chemical properties, they require different manufacturing processes. This is why some communities ask that plastics be sorted into different recycling bins. Emphasize to students that even though plastics may look alike, they are actually quite different.

Have students bring in their clean, empty recyclable plastic materials from home over the course of a week. Sort the plastics according to the numbers printed on them. At the end of the week, have a discussion about the amount of waste materials produced by the households in the class. What can be done to reduce the amount of plastic we use? If desired, ask students to discuss this issue with their families, then share their findings with the class.

Polyethylene terephthalate (PTE) is coded with a

High density polyethylene (HDPE) is coded with a

Resculptures

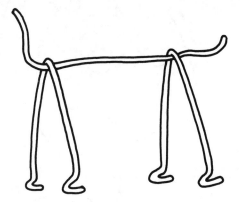

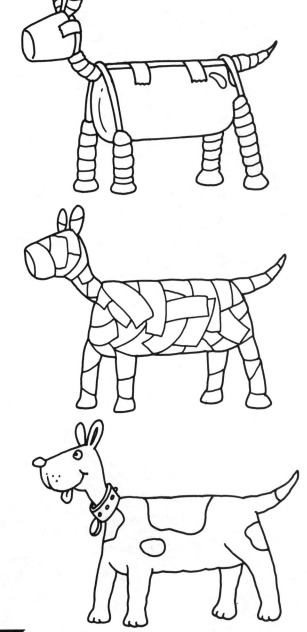

MATERIALS:

a mixture of nonrecycled materials, such as
Styrofoam; #3, #4, and #5 plastic containers;
juice boxes; and milk cartons
wire coat hangers
masking tape
wallpaper paste
newspaper
mixing bowls
paint or clear varnish
paintbrushes

DIRECTIONS:

1. Give each student a selection of nonrecyclable materials. Have each child sketch a sculpture design based on these materials.
2. Tell students to use a wire hanger and masking tape to help hold the sculpture materials in place.
3. Rip strips of newspaper. Mix up small mixing bowls of wallpaper paste and water until the paste begins to thin. Have students use their fingers to coat strips of newspaper with the paste, then lay the strips over their sculpture frames.
4. Students may wish to keep portions of their sculpture frames uncovered so the nonrecycled materials show through.
5. Have each child complete two layers of the newspaper strips, applying the second layer in the opposite direction of the first.
6. When the sculptures dry, let each student apply clear varnish to his or her sculpture. Display the sculptures in the art center under the heading "Recycled Sculptures."

Recycling Scrapbook

MATERIALS:
scissors
glue
12" x 18" construction paper
stapler

DIRECTIONS:
1. Have students create patterns to use in a recycling scrapbook.
2. Encourage students to look through newspapers and magazines each day for articles, pictures, and other information about recycling and the environment. Have students cut out the articles, sort them according to the particular problem they address, and glue them on 12" x 18" construction paper.
3. Ask each student to comment on the situation discussed in each article. Give students several questions to answer about each article, such as:

What do you think is the viewpoint of the writer?
Are there two (or more) opposing sides in this issue?
How does this issue affect the community? Does it
    affect other communities as well?
How do you feel about this issue?

4. Have students attach their essays on facing pages to the articles they have cut out. Then ask each child to place the pages together in order and make a cover and title each book.
5. Staple the books along the left side. Place the scrapbooks in the reading or science center for everyone to see.

Nature-Walk Haikus

Ask if anyone knows what a haiku is. Explain to the class that the haiku is an ancient form of Japanese poetry. Haikus do not rhyme, but they do have a specific structure. The first line of a haiku consists of five syllables, the second line has seven syllables, and the third line has five syllables.

Share some haikus with the class. For example:

> Sky so blue and bright,
> I reach up to touch the sun,
> Warming this grand day.

Tell students that haikus are usually written about subjects in nature. Then take the class outside for a short nature walk. Ask children to bring writing pads and pencils with them to jot down any thoughts they might have.

After returning to the classroom, ask students to write haikus about something they have seen on their walk. If desired, have children illustrate their poems as well. Then attach the poems and illustrations to a bulletin board under the title "Nature-Walk Haikus."

Environmental Word Box

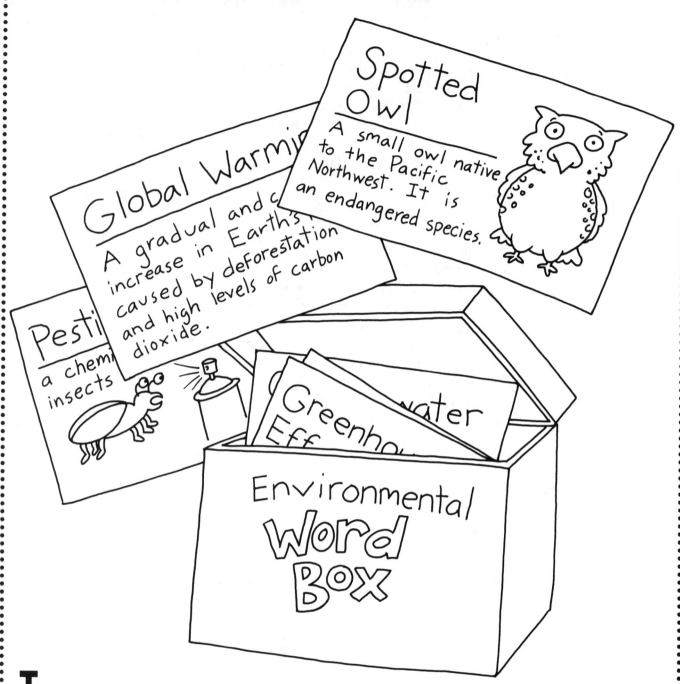

Spotted Owl

A small owl native to the Pacific Northwest. It is an endangered species.

Global Warming

A gradual and c... increase in Earth's ... caused by deforestation and high levels of carbon dioxide.

Pesti...

a chem... insects

Greenhouse Eff...

...ater

Environmental *Word Box*

Tell the class that they will be making an environmental word box. Distribute 5" x 7" index cards to students.

Over the course of a week or two, have students write down vocabulary words having to do with the environment on one side of an index card, one word per index card. On the other side, have them write the definitions of these words.

If desired, ask students to draw small illustrations for words whenever possible.

After the specified amount of time is up, collect all the index cards. Place any duplicate words aside.

Have a small group of students alphabetize the words and place them in a small file box. Encourage students to use the file box as a quick-reference tool when researching environmental or other science projects.

Air Testing

Show students how clean or dirty the air is in their town by performing this experiment. Begin by spreading a thin layer of petroleum jelly on the inside of a clean glass jar.

Place the jar at least 2 feet off the ground in an open area in the schoolyard, away from the playground, athletic fields, or other areas that have frequent traffic.
After two days, send a small group of students out to observe the jar. Has any dirt appeared?

Send another group out two days later to make further observations.

Several days later, bring the jar back into the classroom. Ask volunteers to examine the jar and comment. How much dirt is on the jar? What kind of dirt does it look like? Ask students what they think might have caused the dirt in the air.

Make a Difference

Name _____

If you want to help the environment, write a letter to a national or local elected official about an issue that is important to you. Be sure to use the correct form when writing a business letter. Here's an example:

January 20, 1996 (date)

President of the United States (name of recipient)
The White House (address of recipient)
1600 Pennsylvania Avenue
Washington, DC 20500

Dear Mr. President: (greeting)

     I am writing to you because I am concerned about the amount of pollution in the ocean. I live near a beach, and we were unable to swim in the ocean several times last summer because of garbage in the water.

     I would like to know what is being done to prevent this type of pollution from happening again. Please let me know what I can do to help.

Sincerely, (closing)
Robert Murphy (signature)

Robert Murphy

If you would like to write to a member of the United States Senate, use this address:

The Honorable (name of senator)
U.S. Senate
Washington, DC 20510

If you would like to write to a member of the U.S. House of Representatives, use this address:

The Honorable (name of representative)
U.S. House of Representatives
Washington, DC 20515

Environmental Organizations

For help in locating information about various environmental issues, contact some of the organizations listed below.

Alliance to Save Energy
1725 K Street, Suite 914
Washington, DC 20006

Center for Action on Endangered Species
175 West Main Street
Ayer, MA 01432

Clean Water Action
317 Pennsylvania Avenue, S.E.
Washington, DC 20003

Environmental Action Coalition
625 Broadway
New York, NY 10012

Environmental Defense Fund
257 Park Avenue South
New York, NY 10010

Friends of the Earth
218 D Street
Washington, DC 20003

Greenpeace
1611 Connecticut Avenue, N.W.
Washington, DC 20009

The Humane Society of the United States
2100 L Street, N.W.
Washington, DC 20037

Environmental Organizations

Keep America Beautiful
9 West Broad Street
Greenwich, CT 06892

National Audubon Society
950 Third Avenue
New York, NY 10022

National Recycling Coalition
1101 30th Street, N.W.
Washington, DC 20007

National Wildlife Federation
1412 16th Street, N.W.
Washington, DC 20036

Renew America
1400 16th Street, Suite 710
Washington, DC 20036

Sierra Club
730 Polk Street
San Francisco, CA 94109

Solar Energy Research Institute
1617 Cole Boulevard
Golden, CO 80401

U.S. Environmental Protection Agency (EPA)
401 M Street, S.W.
A 108
Washington, DC 20460

World Wildlife Fund
P.O. Box 96220
Washington, DC 20077-7787

Toxic Alert

Name _____

Read the list of toxic substances below. Then look in your home to see which of these chemicals your family uses. Put a check in the box next to each item.

☐ bleach   ☐ insect spray

☐ drain cleaner   ☐ laundry detergent

☐ epoxy   ☐ nail-polish remover

☐ floor wax   ☐ paint thinner

☐ furniture polish   ☐ rodent poison

☐ glass cleaner   ☐ turpentine

☐ hair spray

Can you think of environmentally safe products that may be used in place of these materials? Write your suggestions on the lines below.

_____   _____

_____   _____

_____   _____

_____   _____

_____   _____

Water Watch

Name _____

Fill in the number of gallons of water you think it usually takes to perform each of the tasks below.

_____ gallons

_____ gallons

_____ gallons

_____ gallons

_____ gallons

_____ gallons

_____ gallons

_____ gallons

_____ gallons

Can you think of some ways to cut down on water use? Write your suggestions on a separate piece of paper.

Earth Day Celebrations

Ask if anyone knows what Earth Day is. Explain to students that Earth Day was first celebrated on April 22, 1972, as a way to focus attention on our planet.

Brainstorm with the class to think of some special ways to celebrate Earth Day. Some suggestions are:

Hold an Earth Day fair. Invite friends, families, and other classes to listen to speeches, read newsletters, or participate in science demonstrations, or other interesting events.

Obtain permission for the class to plant a tree in a local area.

Work together to clean up a local park, river, beach, or other public area.

Create an "Earth Day Activity Book" for students in the lower grades. Include mazes, word searches, crossword puzzles, stories, and other fun activities with an environmental theme.

Find out about your school's recycling program. See what can be done to improve it!

Ask each student to bring in one or two paperback books from home to trade in a book swap. Recycled literature can be lots of fun!

Have students write stories about what they hope the world will be like in 100 years.

You may also wish to make the Earth Cake recipe on page 11 as a special treat for all to enjoy.

Glossary

acid rain precipitation that is unusually high in sulfuric and nitric acid content caused by industrial pollution

battery a device that generates an electric current by chemical reaction

biodegradable capable of being decomposed by a natural process

biome a community of living organisms within a large ecological region

carbon dioxide a gas formed during respiration, combustion, and organic decomposition

carnivore a meat-eating or predatory organism

chlorofluorocarbon (CFC) compound that is used in aerosols and refrigerants

compost a mixture of decaying organic matter that may be used for fertilizer

decompose to separate into small parts; to rot

decomposer an agent, such as bacteria, that helps break down a material into small parts

deforestation the clearing away of trees and forests

disposable designed to be thrown away after use

ecology the science of the relationships between organisms and their environments

ecosystem a community of organisms and the environment in which they interact

endangered species specific animals, insects, or plants that are decreasing in numbers and are in danger of becoming extinct

energy heat or electric power

environment all living things and their surroundings

erosion a natural process in which material is removed from the Earth's surface

extinct no longer existing on Earth

fossil fuel natural substance, such as coal and oil, that is deep inside Earth and may be burned to release energy

global warming a gradual and continuing increase in Earth's temperature; caused by deforestation and high levels of carbon dioxide

greenhouse effect a gradual, steady increase in Earth's temperature caused by gases trapped by Earth's atmosphere

groundwater water sources that lie under the ground

Glossary

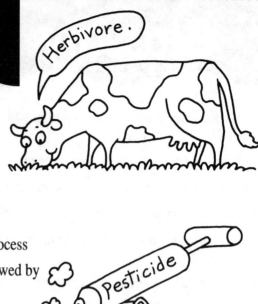
Herbivore.

habitat   the area in which an organism naturally lives

herbivore   a plant-eating animal

kilowatt   a unit of measure for electricity

landfill   a large hole in which garbage is buried under layers of dirt

litter   rubbish that has been discarded carelessly

nonbiodegradable   incapable of being decomposed by a natural process

nonrenewable resource   a resource that cannot be replaced or renewed by humans or by natural processes

Pesticide

nuclear energy   the energy released by a nuclear reaction

organic   coming from living organisms

oxygen   a gas that is essential for plant and animal respiration as well as most combustion processes

ozone layer   a layer of oxygen that surrounds Earth and protects organisms from the sun's ultraviolet rays

pesticide   a chemical that is used to kill insects and rodents

petroleum   a natural liquid found beneath the earth's surface that is used for natural gas, fuel oil, and other products

phosphate   a chemical compound, containing phosphorus and oxygen, that is necessary to the growth of plants and animals

photosynthesis   the process by which green plants convert light to energy and release oxygen

pollutant   something that contaminates soil, water, or air

Pollutant

rain forest   a dense, tropical forest near the equator

recycle   to produce useful materials from garbage or waste

resource   substance available to help human life

solar energy   energy that comes from the sun

toxic   harmful or deadly

ultraviolet radiation   radiation that comes from the sun

wetland   a lowland area filled with moisture, such as a marsh or swamp

Solar energy.

page 5

```
U R C O N S T E L L A T I O N S P R
T E T Z A S T R A U T R M B R L Y O
U M U U P T Z G A R O C E O U X S P
A O A K C O M A R S T U N I T B T H
N N N R A T M O O A D H G K A I I K
U O O A B U D N S U V E N U S G R Y
T R E T I P U J U P L I T O M J E J
O T R Y G S O O R X H A T M I T O I
I S T T D M H T A G A E X Y L M I G
B A S T R O T E N A L P R M K L R P
C I A I Q O E C U E S U J E Y A S L
J Y G B U T U L S L P L U T W T G A
L T P D X A N C Y E F T B R A I N T
D U L O I N O O M E R C U R Y P D U
O F A L C P L U I T O R A N H L M P
C E R R E P P I L G I B T R E U B S
B I G D I P P E R T U A N O R T S A
G R V A Y X Y H Y X A L A G O O N M
```

page 9

```
                    ¹W
              ²L A N D          ³D
                    T          E
          ⁴O N E    ⁵M    ⁶R E V O L V E
          X        O          E
          Y        U          R
    ⁷R    G        N          T
  ⁸F O R E S T S   T          S
    T    N        A          ⁹G
    A        ¹⁰G L A C I E R S
    T             N          A
    I             S          V
    O                        I
  ¹¹S U N      ¹²P          T
              O          Y
         ¹³M I L K Y W A Y
  ¹⁴C    L
¹⁵C O N T I N E N T A L D R I F T
  R    U
  E    ¹⁶C O P E R N I C U S
         I
         O
```

page 26

Answers will vary for the first part. Possible answers include:
On the farm: fertilizers causing pollution; erosion of soil
In the home: detergents and fertilizers causing pollution
At the power plant: thermal pollution
At the chemical plant: chemical pollution causing destruction of
    natural habitats and the ozone
At the landfill: garbage polluting soil and water supplies from seepage
At the water treatment plant: untreated sewage getting through and
polluting the water supply

Answers will vary for the second part.

page 27

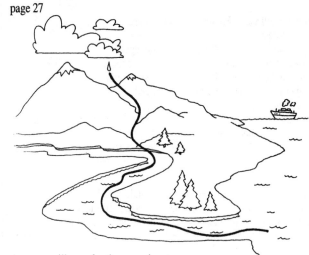

Answers will vary for the second part.

page 33

1. c   5. h
2. g   6. b
3. a   7. d
4. e   8. f

page 35

1. sunlight   4. water
2. chloroplast   5. sugar
3. carbon dioxide 6. oxygen

page 38

```
                  ¹C
                  R          ²L
              ³R H I N O C E R O S        ⁴S
                  E          O          N
                  ⁵C H ⁶E E T A H        A
                       L          R      I
                       E          D      L
                 ⁷B    P                 D
                 A     H                 A
              ⁸B L U E W H A L E         R
                 D     A          ¹⁰O    T
           ⁹C    E     N          S      E
           O     A     T          ¹¹T I G E R
           U     G                R
          ¹²G O R I L L A         I
           A     E                ¹³C O N D O R
           R
```

Answers

page 41

Answers will vary. Possible answers include:
1. rain forest
2. plants/insects/parrot; plants/monkey/leopard
3. trees depend on rain for growth/animals depend on air to breathe
4. loss of homes for animals/loss of food for animals/weather patterns in other parts of the world may be changed forever
5. A pond; a desert
6. I need air to breathe, water to drink, plants and animals to eat, trees for shade and shelter, stores to buy clothing and food, library for books, school for an education, car or bus for transportation

page 42

Answers will vary. Possible answers include:
1. The squirrel and bird live in the tree; the fish live in the river; the worms live in the log and in the ground; the birds eat the worms; the squirrels eat the nuts from the tree; the fish eat little organisms that live in the river.
2. The mouse lives in the hole; the roots of the cactus hold water to nourish the plant and the animals; the snake eats the mouse; the coyote eats the bird; the mouse eats the ants.

page 43

1. d	5. e	9. m	13. i
2. a	6. f	10. k	
3. b	7. h	11. j	
4. c	8. g	12. l	

page 45

1. element	6. compound
2. mixture	7. mixture
3. compound	8. element
4. element	9. compound
5. compound	10. mixture

page 46

Answers will vary. Possible answers include:
bicycle: wheel, axle, lever, gears
egg beater: gears
clothesline: pulleys
playground slide: inclined plane
auger: screw
sewing needle: wedge
wheelbarrow: lever, wheel, axle

page 51–52

Answers will vary. Possible answers include:
1. mechanical energy (garbage truck, snowblower); electric energy (toaster; hair dryer; fan; lamp; microwave; radio); radiant energy (sun)
2. garbage truck and snowblower
3. Sarah's voice
4. No. The cold air generated by the fan takes longer to dry Sarah's hair than the hot air generated by a blow dryer.
5. The warmth of the sun is absorbed by the window glass and warms the room.
6. To provide radiant energy (light) for the plants so that they can carry out photosynthesis.
7. Using a snow shovel.

page 53

Answers will vary. Possible answers include:

2		room air conditioner—clean the air filter regularly
9	X	electric carving knife—use a regular carving knife
4	X	dishwasher—only wash full loads of dishes
6		microwave oven—cook several foods at the same time
7		radio—turn it off when you have finished listening to it
1		refrigerator/freezer (14 cubic feet)—keep doors closed
3		color television (tube type)—turn TV off when you are done watching it
10	X	electric toothbrush—brush your teeth with a regular toothbrush several times a week
8	X	vacuum cleaner—vacuum once a week, not every day
5		washing machine (automatic)—only wash full loads of laundry

page 54

Answers will vary for solutions.

page 57

Answers will vary for the second part of this exercise. Possible answers include: Turn down the stereo, turn off the TV, use a carpet sweep instead of a vacuum, use a rake instead of a leaf blower.

Answers

page 61

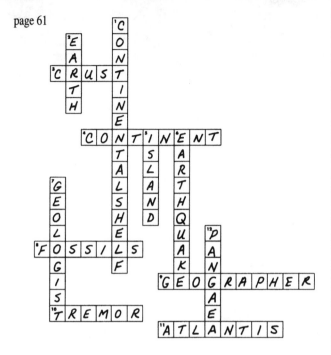

page 64

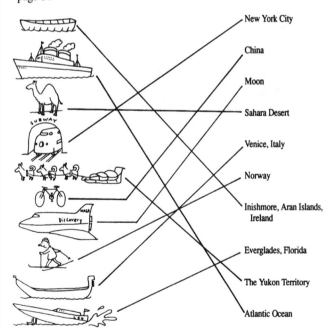

New York City

China

Moon

Sahara Desert

Venice, Italy

Norway

Inishmore, Aran Islands, Ireland

Everglades, Florida

The Yukon Territory

Atlantic Ocean

page 67

Renewable sources: ethanol, nuclear, solar, windmill, tidal, water
Nonrenewable: petroleum, coal, natural gas, wood, animal, oil, kerosene, diesel

page 68

Answers

page 69

Answers will vary. Possible answers include:
1. lunch bag made of reusable thermal material; hard plastic container to hold a sandwich and snack
2. cloth bag; mesh or net carrying bag
3. wooden crates or plastic crates
4. glasses or plastic cups
5. ceramic coffee mugs or cups; thermal cups
6. cloth napkins
7. reusable aluminum, metal, or glass roasting pans
8. plastic or glass storage containers with lids
9. cloth diapers
10. hard plastic plates or glass plates

page 75

Toxic waste: battery, paint thinner, broken radio
Recyclable waste: juice box, cardboard hamburger package, can, bottle, newspaper, plastic soda bottle, broken window
Compostable waste: grass, leaves, tree branches, vegetables scraps
Nonrecyclable garbage: broken dish, book, chicken bones

page 76

Answers will vary. Possible answers include:
1. Trees—Alternate recycling source: newspapers/magazines/cardboard. Advantage of recycling: saves trees, increases forestation, keeps environment cleaner
2. Iron ore—Alternate recycling source: steel cans. Advantage of recycling: less pollution, conserves energy
3. Sand—Alternate recycling source: glass jars and bottles. Advantage of recycling: natural resources not depleted, conserves energy
4. Oil—Alternate recycling source: plastic bottles and containers. Advantage of recycling: time savings, less pollution because oil doesn't have to be drilled
5. Bauxite ore—Alternate recycling source: aluminum cans. Advantage of recycling: less pollution, mines do not have to be dug, so it's better for the environment, conserves energy.

page 77

Answers will vary. Possible answers include:
1. Glass jars and bottles: windows, pottery, eyeglasses, drinking glasses, mirrors, light bulbs
2. Steel cans: paper clips, kitchen appliances, razor blades
3. Aluminum cans: aluminum foil, window frames, telephone wires, license plates, chewing gum wrappers
4. Newspapers: paper napkins, paper towels, cereal boxes
5. White paper: stationery, white envelopes
6. Plastic: plastic bags, toys, containers, contact lenses

page 87

Answers will vary.

page 88

Answers will vary.